# THE ESSENTIAL
# LOW CHOLESTEROL
# COOKBOOK

**Enjoy Tasty and Heart-Healthy Recipes for Daily Wellness and Cholesterol Reduction — Includes a 28-Day Meal Plan, Weekly Shopping Lists & Colorful Food Photos**

## Danny Gibson

**2025**

# TABLE OF CONTENTS

## CHAPTER 4. SOUPS    31

## CHAPTER 6. MEAT & POULTRY    45

## CHAPTER 5. FISH & SEAFOOD    37

## CHAPTER 7. SIDE DISHES & VEGGIES    53

## CHAPTER 8. SNACKS & DRINKS — 61

## CHAPTER 9. 28-DAY MEAL PLAN — 71

## CONCLUSION — 82

# INTRODUCTION
## YOUR JOURNEY TO A HEALTHIER HEART STARTS HERE

*Dear reader,* Let me tell you something right from the heart—literally. I know what it's like to hear the words "your cholesterol is too high" during a doctor's visit. I remember the wave of concern that followed. The questions. The doubt. And above all, the desire to fix it without giving up the joy of food or the hope for a healthier future.

### YOU'RE NOT ALONE!

If you've just been diagnosed, or if you've been managing high cholesterol for a while, I want you to know: you're not alone. I've been where you are. I've felt that mix of frustration and confusion. And I've learned—through research, trial and error, and a lot of meals—that there's a better way forward.

**This book is for anyone who has been told their cholesterol is too high, has a family history of heart disease, or simply wants to take control of their long-term health through smarter nutrition.**

Whether you're in your 30s and thinking preventively, or in your 60s managing existing risks, the low-cholesterol diet offers a powerful, science-backed path to lasting well-being.

### A REAL-WORLD, HEART-FIRST APPROACH

When I first started changing the way I ate, I felt like I had to choose between food I enjoyed and food that was "allowed."

But what I discovered is this: a low-cholesterol diet doesn't have to be bland or restrictive.

With the right ingredients, thoughtful swaps, and a little guidance, you can still love what's on your plate—and support your heart at the same time. This isn't just about numbers on a chart.

**It's about waking up with more energy, feeling good after meals, and knowing you're doing something kind for your body every single day!**

### WHAT YOU'LL FIND INSIDE

To make things as easy and sustainable as possible, I've **included a complete 28-Day Meal Plan** along with **Weekly Shopping Lists**. I know how overwhelming it can be to change your eating habits, especially at the beginning. These tools provide a roadmap and help you build stick habits.

You won't find fad diet gimmicks here—just nourishing meals built on solid science and real-life experience: simple food that supports your heart.

### FROM ONE HEART TO ANOTHER

You don't need to do this alone. I wrote this book because I wish I'd had something like it when I was starting out—something honest, encouraging, and practical. If I could lower my cholesterol and feel better without giving up the joy of food, so can you.

### LET'S TAKE THIS ONE STEP AT A TIME, TOGETHER!

*Warmly, Danny Gibson!*

# CHAPTER 1
# BASICS OF THE DIET
## UNDERSTANDING CHOLESTEROL: FRIEND OR FOE?

### MAKING SENSE OF CHOLESTEROL

Cholesterol has a complicated reputation. It's often blamed for heart attacks and clogged arteries, but your body needs cholesterol to function correctly.

It's a waxy, fat-like substance found in every cell, helping build hormones and vitamin D and aiding digestion. The issue isn't cholesterol itself but rather its type and balance.

- **LDL (Low-Density Lipoprotein)** – Often labeled as "bad" cholesterol, LDL carries cholesterol through your bloodstream. When present in excess, it tends to deposit on the walls of your arteries, contributing to plaque buildup and narrowing of the vessels. This can increase the risk of heart disease, stroke, and inflammation.
- **HDL (High-Density Lipoprotein)** – Known as the "good" cholesterol, HDL acts as a cleanup crew. It collects excess cholesterol and transports it back to your liver for removal. Higher levels of HDL cholesterol are associated with a lower risk of cardiovascular disease.

Maintaining the right balance between LDL and HDL cholesterol helps keep your heart healthy.

### WHY CHOLESTEROL BALANCE MATTERS

Cholesterol is not inherently dangerous, but imbalanced levels are. Your cardiovascular system is stressed when your LDL levels are high and your HDL levels are low.

Over time, this imbalance leads to atherosclerosis, a condition in which arteries harden and narrow, making blood flow more difficult.

1. Support **normal hormone production**
2. Protect **arteries from damage and inflammation**
3. Help maintain **healthy blood pressure and circulation**

In contrast, poor cholesterol levels may go unnoticed for years, until a major health issue appears. That's why prevention is key, primarily through what you eat daily.

### DIET: THE MOST POWERFUL TOOL YOU HAVE

The good news? **Cholesterol levels are highly responsive to changes in diet.** You don't need to rely solely on medication. Many people can improve their numbers significantly through food choices alone. A heart-friendly diet focuses on:

- **Reducing saturated fats and trans fats**
- **Increasing fiber from whole plant foods**
- **Incorporating healthy fats from**
- **nuts, seeds, and fish**
- **Eating more colorful, antioxidant-rich vegetables and fruits**

These shifts help lower LDL levels, raise HDL levels, and improve heart health.

I know what it's like to get a test result that says, "You have high cholesterol." I've been there myself. But when I started changing my diet, things gradually began to improve. Most importantly, I felt I was in control of my life.

### THIS BOOK IS DESIGNED TO HELP YOU FEEL CONFIDENT, TOO.

# BUILDING THE FOUNDATION: CORE PRINCIPLES

When I was first told my cholesterol levels were too high, I felt confused and overwhelmed. I thought I was eating "healthy"—but the numbers told another story. That moment pushed me to explore what works. I found that lowering cholesterol doesn't mean eating less—it means eating smarter.

Decades of research and clinical evidence support the low-cholesterol diet and its sustainable choices that benefit your heart and blood vessels.

## 1. REDUCE SATURATED FATS — ELIMINATE TRANS FATS

**Saturated fats,** commonly found in red meat, butter, cheese, and processed foods, raise LDL ("bad") cholesterol in the blood. Numerous studies have linked a high intake of saturated fats to increased risk of heart disease. While you don't have to eliminate them, reducing them is a proven way to improve your lipid profile.

**Trans fats,** on the other hand, should be avoided entirely. They're artificial fats that extend the shelf life in baked goods and fried foods. Even small amounts can raise LDL, lower HDL ("good") cholesterol, and contribute to inflammation and arterial damage.

**Scientific Note:** According to the American Heart Association, trans fats are so harmful that many countries have banned them entirely. Even if labels say "0g trans fat," double-check for ingredients like "partially hydrogenated oils."

## 2. INCREASE SOLUBLE FIBER AND UNSATURATED FATS

Soluble fiber acts like a sponge in your digestive tract. It binds to cholesterol and facilitates its removal from the body.

At the same time, replace saturated fats with **unsaturated fats**, particularly those rich in omega-3 fatty acids. In **fatty fish**, omega-3s lower blood pressure and improve overall heart health.

**Scientific Note:** Studies published in journals like Circulation and The Lancet support the cardioprotective effects of fiber and unsaturated fats, showing improved cholesterol levels within weeks of dietary changes.

## 3. EAT MORE WHOLE, PLANT-BASED FOODS

Whole, unprocessed plant foods contain **fiber, antioxidants, and phytosterols** that help reduce inflammation and support healthy cholesterol levels. To boost heart health and energy, fill half your plate with vegetables and fruits and choose **whole grains, legumes, and nuts** over refined foods.

**Scientific Note:** A review in the American Journal of Clinical Nutrition found that replacing just 15–20% of calories from refined carbs with legumes or whole grains can significantly improve cholesterol ratios in as little as 8 weeks.

## 4. MODERATE ANIMAL PRODUCTS — CHOOSE LEAN

Animal products can be part of a heart-healthy diet if chosen wisely. Opt **for lean meats, skinless poultry, low-fat dairy products, and omega-3 rich fish.** Limit **processed meats**, and enjoy eggs in moderation—preferably with fiber-rich sides.

You'll eat better, feel better, and see real results.

### YOUR HEART IS WORTH THE EFFORT, BECAUSE EVERY BITE MATTERS!

# FOODS THAT HELP LOWER CHOLESTEROL

What you choose to put on your plate can have a powerful effect on your cholesterol levels, often more than you might expect.

Instead of focusing only on what to cut out, the Low Cholesterol Diet encourages you to add more foods that support heart health, improve cholesterol balance, and reduce inflammation.

## OATS AND WHOLE GRAINS

Oats are one of the most studied and reliable foods for lowering cholesterol. They're rich in **beta-glucan**, a type of soluble fiber that binds to cholesterol in the digestive tract and helps eliminate it from the body before it enters the bloodstream.

Adding just one bowl of oatmeal per day (about 3 grams of soluble fiber) has been shown to reduce LDL levels by up to 5–10%.

**Start your morning with savory mushroom oatmeal with poached eggs**

Top soluble fiber sources: quinoa, lentils, oats, wild rice, beans, and almond flour.

## FATTY FISH: RICH IN HEART-HEALTHY OMEGA-3S

Fatty fish such as **salmon** are high in omega-3 fatty acids—essential fats that help reduce triglycerides, lower inflammation, and improve the overall lipid profile.

While omega-3s don't directly lower LDL, they help stabilize the heart, improve blood vessel function, and reduce the risk of plaque buildup.

**Bake a grilled salmon with vegetables for a heart-smart dinner**

Aim for two servings per week of fatty fish prepared by grilling, baking, or steaming — not frying.

## OLIVE OIL: LIQUID GOLD FOR THE HEART

Olive oil, especially **extra virgin olive oil**, is packed with monounsaturated fats and powerful antioxidants called **polyphenols**. Olive oil also reduces oxidative stress and improves the function of the endothelium (the inner lining of blood vessels), which is a key factor in preventing atherosclerosis.

**Use olive oil as a base for a salad with avocado and feta**

Use olive oil as your main cooking fat or in salad dressings, dips, and marinades.

## APPLES, PEARS, AND CITRUS: PECTIN PROVIDERS

**Apples, pears and oranges** are rich in pectin — a soluble fiber that helps remove cholesterol and supports heart health.

**Enjoy a baked pear with cheese or carrot and orange smoothie**

Pectin slows digestion, helps regulate blood sugar, and feeds beneficial gut bacteria—all connected to better cholesterol control.

## BEANS AND LENTILS: PLANT-BASED PROTEIN

**Legumes** such as **beans, lentils, and chickpeas** are cholesterol-lowering superstars. They're high in soluble and insoluble fiber and provide a steady, plant-based source of protein.

Regularly consuming legumes has been linked to lower LDL cholesterol levels and improved blood sugar management.

**Prepare delicious lentil patties for a filling, protein-rich, and energizing breakfast**

Swap animal proteins a few times weekly for hearty plant-based options like tomato bean soup, lentil patties, or chickpea curry.

# FOODS TO AVOID FOR LOWER CHOLESTEROL

While adding heart-healthy foods to your diet is a crucial step, knowing what to reduce or eliminate is equally important.

Some foods — primarily those high in saturated fats, trans fats, added sugars, and refined carbs — can raise LDL ("bad") cholesterol, increase inflammation, and contribute to plaque buildup in the arteries. Here are the top foods to limit or avoid, along with healthier alternatives:

## HIGH-FAT MEATS AND PROCESSED MEATS

Fatty cuts of red meat, such as ribs, pork belly, and heavily marbled beef, as well as sausages, bacon, salami, and deli meats, are high in saturated fat and sodium. Regular consumption has been linked to increased cardiovascular risk.

**Choose lean cuts like skinless poultry, turkey breast, or plant-based protein.**

## FULL-FAT DAIRY PRODUCTS

Whole milk, butter, and high-fat cheeses are significant contributors to saturated fat. While dairy can still be part of a heart-healthy diet, opting for low-fat or fat-free versions is a better choice. They provide essential nutrients- calcium and protein—without extra saturated fat.

**Opt for skim and almond milk or plant-based alternatives free from added sugars.**

## EGG YOLKS IN EXCESS

Eggs have long been debated for their cholesterol content. Recent studies suggest that moderate egg consumption is safe for most people, but those with elevated cholesterol or a higher risk of heart disease may benefit from limiting yolks.

**Try using more egg whites in recipes, or pair whole eggs with fiber-rich foods like vegetables or whole grains.**

## FOODS WITH INDUSTRIAL TRANS FATS

Artificial trans fats are among the most detrimental fats for heart health. Common in margarine, shelf-stable baked goods, packaged snacks, and fried foods, trans fats increase LDL and lower HDL ("good") cholesterol.

**Always check labels for "partially hydrogenated oils" and avoid them altogether.**

## SUGARY DRINKS AND ULTRA-PROCESSED FOODS

Soda, sweetened coffee drinks, and processed baked goods (cookies, pastries, snack cakes) may not contain cholesterol. Still, they promote insulin resistance, inflammation, and weight gain—all of which affect your heart health.

**Choose water, herbal teas, or unsweetened sparkling water. For sweets, make your own using natural ingredients and healthy fats.**

# HOW TO COOK DELICIOUS AND HEALTHY MEALS

When it comes to heart health and cholesterol balance, how you cook your meals is just as essential as what you put on your plate.

The proper techniques preserve nutrients and bring out the natural flavor of whole foods, without the need for excess salt, unhealthy fats, or overly processed sauces.

### INNOVATIVE COOKING METHODS

Skip the deep fryer and opt for healthier, more gentle cooking methods that support your goals:

- **Bake, steam, grill, or braise** your food to retain texture and flavor with minimal added fat.
- **Boil or roast vegetables** to enhance their natural sweetness.
- **Avoid deep-frying** and cooking with butter or cream-based sauces, as they contain saturated fats.

These techniques help reduce your intake of harmful fats while still delivering satisfying and delicious results.

### FLAVOR FIRST

Reducing sodium is vital for managing blood pressure, especially since high blood pressure often goes hand in hand with elevated cholesterol and increased cardiovascular risk.

To add flavor without relying on salt:

- Use fresh herbs **like basil, parsley,** or **thyme.**
- Add acidity with **lemon juice** or **zest** for a bright finish.
- Spice things up with **paprika, cumin, turmeric,** or **chili flakes.**

### INSPIRATION IN EVERY RECIPE

Each recipe in this book is simple, flavorful, and supports your heart health goals. With easy techniques, accessible ingredients, and a 28-day meal plan, you'll confidently build healthy habits. Let's quickly recap what we've covered in a simple, at-a-glance format. The table below outlines which foods to prioritize and which to limit or avoid if you aim to support healthier cholesterol levels and overall heart health.

### PRACTICAL GUIDELINES

By cutting back on foods that harm your cholesterol profile and embracing more whole, heart-loving options, you're investing in long-term health, vitality, and energy.

| Foods to Embrace More Often | Foods Best Minimized or Avoided |
|---|---|
| Oats, barley, quinoa, and whole-grain breads | Full-fat dairy (butter, cream, high-fat cheese) |
| Almonds, walnuts (in moderation) | Fatty red meats and organ meats |
| Avocados | Processed meats (sausages, bacon, deli cuts) |
| Fresh vegetables of all kinds | Refined grains, white bread, and pastries |
| Fruits high in pectin (apples, pears, citrus) | Fried foods, chips, and salty snacks |
| Fatty fish 2–3 times a week | Palm and coconut oil in excess |
| Legumes like lentils, chickpeas, and black beans | Any product with "partially hydrogenated oils" |

This book includes a shopping list and a step-by-step meal plan to simplify things. You can implement these changes immediately without second-guessing or overthinking.

# SIMPLE STEPS TO TRANSFORM YOUR LIFESTYLE

First, I would like to congratulate you on choosing a path that prioritizes your health and well-being. You've already taken an incredible step by picking up this book and committing to a diet that supports your heart. Your decision to make healthier choices now will have long-term benefits, and I'm here to help you every step of the way.

As you move forward, it's important to remember that a healthy heart isn't just about what we eat—it's about the lifestyle we lead. This chapter will guide you through simple yet powerful lifestyle changes that complement your heart-healthy diet and help you achieve your goals.

## 1 MOVEMENT: MAKE 30 MINUTES OF ACTIVITY A DAILY HABIT

No matter how busy life gets, try to carve out at least 30 minutes daily for physical activity.

Whether it's a brisk walk, cycling, dancing, or yoga, regular physical activity is one of the best things you can do for your heart.

It boosts circulation, helps manage cholesterol levels, reduces stress, and energizes the body. It's all about consistency, not perfection—so find what works for you and stick with it.

## 2 SAY NO TO SMOKING AND LIMIT ALCOHOL

Avoiding smoking and keeping alcohol intake to minimum is vital for heart health. Smoking accelerates the development of plaque in your arteries, increasing the risk of heart disease.

Excessive alcohol consumption can raise blood pressure and lead to weight gain, both of which strain your heart. By making these simple changes you're giving your heart the best chance to thrive.

## 3 MANAGE YOUR WEIGHT AND STRESS LEVELS

Maintaining a healthy weight and learning to manage stress are crucial for keeping your cholesterol level within a healthy range and reducing your risk of heart disease. Even small weight reductions can have a profound effect on your heart health.

Stress management—whether through meditation, deep breathing, or engaging in hobbies—also plays a significant role in lowering inflammation and supporting overall heart function.

Remember, it's not about making drastic changes overnight. Small, consistent steps will add up over time. As you explore the delicious and heart healthy recipes in the next chapter, remember that they are designed to nourish your body, improve your cholesterol levels, and help you feel your best.

I'm thrilled to join your journey toward a healthier heart. Enjoy the recipes, the cooking process, and the satisfaction of knowing that every meal you prepare is a step toward a longer, healthier life. Continue following the meal plan and adjust it to suit your individual needs.

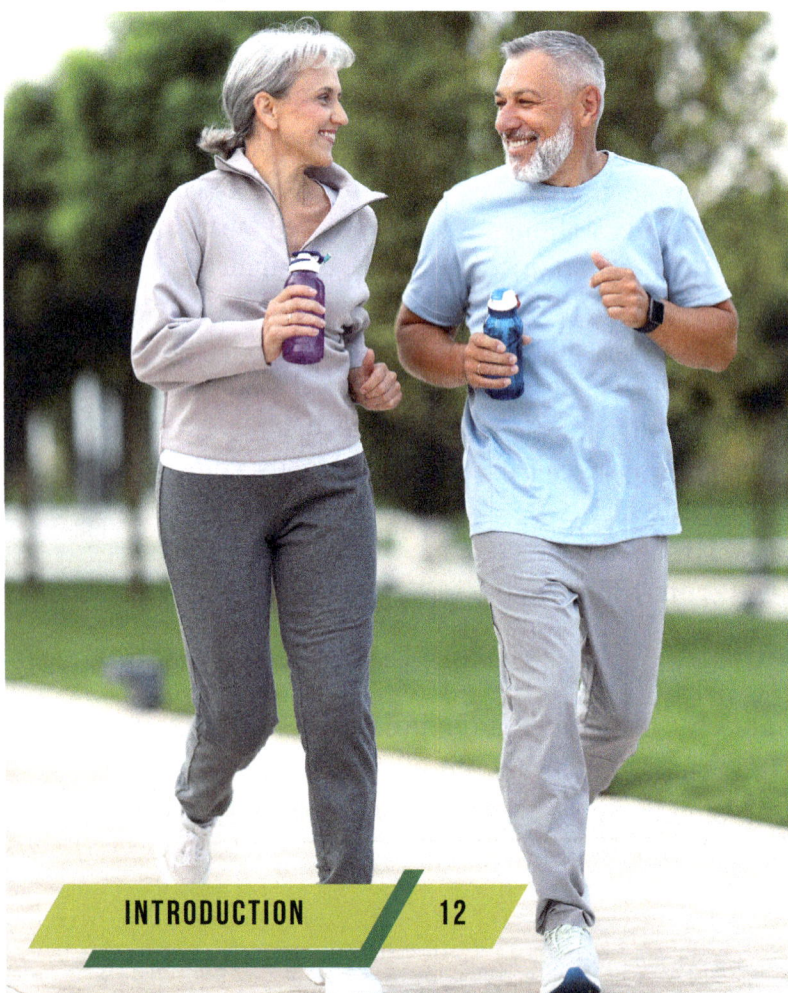

**WISHING YOU DELICIOUS MEALS, HAPPY COOKING AND A HEART THAT FEELS AS GOOD AS IT LOOKS!**

# CHAPTER 2 — BREAKFAST

# DELICIOUS LENTIL PATTIES

**4 Portion  Medium  10 min  20 min**

## INGREDIENTS:

- 250 ml (1 cup) lentils
- 500 ml (2 cups) water
- 1 medium carrot, grated
- 2 garlic cloves, minced
- 1.5 g (1/4 teaspoon) turmeric
- Salt and black pepper, to taste
- 1 bunch of fresh herbs, chopped
- 2 tablespoons (16 g) gluten-free flour

## INSTRUCTIONS:

1. Sort and rinse the lentils thoroughly. Soak them in cold water for at least 2–3 hours or overnight. Drain and rinse again after soaking.
2. Place the lentils in a pot, add 500 ml (2 cups) of water, and bring to a boil. Reduce the heat and simmer for 15–20 minutes, or until the vegetables are tender. Add salt and black pepper 5 minutes before the dish is finished. Remove from the heat and allow to cool slightly.
3. While the lentils cook, finely chop the garlic and herbs, and grate the carrot. Heat a small amount of oil in a skillet and sauté the garlic, carrot, and herbs for 5 minutes, stirring constantly.
4. Combine the cooked lentils with the sautéed vegetables in a bowl. Add turmeric, salt, black pepper, and herbs. Mix thoroughly and refrigerate the mixture for 10–15 minutes to facilitate easier shaping.
5. Shape the mixture into patties, ensuring they have a flat, uniform shape. Heat a skillet over medium heat and lightly coat it with oil. Fry the patties for 2 minutes on each side until golden brown, or bake them in the oven at 180°C (350°F) for 15–20 minutes. Serve warm with your favorite garnish.

**PER SERVING:**
Calories: 180 kcal; Fats: 2g; Protein: 9g; Carbs: 30g; Sugar: 5g; Fiber: 6g

# ROLL SALTED SALMON AND SPINACH

## INGREDIENTS:

- 4 large eggs
- 1 cup (30 g) fresh spinach
- 100 g (3.5 ounces) salted salmon, thinly sliced
- 100 g (3.5 ounces) cream cheese
- 15 ml (1 tablespoon) lemon juice
- Salt and pepper, to taste
- Fresh basil (for garnish)

## INSTRUCTIONS:

1. In a blender, combine eggs, spinach, salt, and pepper. Blend until smooth and evenly mixed. Heat a non-stick skillet over medium heat. Pour half the egg mixture into the skillet, swirling gently to create an even layer. Cook until fully set, about 3–4 minutes, then transfer to a plate. Repeat the process with the remaining mixture.
2. Spread cream cheese evenly over each egg pancake. Add thin slices of salted salmon on top and drizzle with lemon juice.
3. Roll each pancake tightly, then slice the rolls into bite-sized pieces. Garnish with fresh basil before serving.

## PER SERVING:

Calories: 250 kcal; Fats: 17g; Protein: 20g; Carbs: 2g; Sugar: 1g; Fiber: 1g

2 Portion   Easy   10 min   15 min

2 Portion   Easy   10 min   15 min

# MILK BERRY BUCKWHEAT PORRIDGE

## INGREDIENTS:

- 80 g (1/2 cup) buckwheat groats, dry
- 300 ml (1 1/3 cup) low-fat milk
- 160 ml (2/3 cup) water
- 4 fresh strawberries, chopped
- 10 fresh raspberries
- 20 fresh blueberries
- 30 g (2 tablespoons) raisins, pre-soaked
- 10 ml (2 teaspoons) cream (10%), for garnish
- Sweetener (optional), to taste
- Cinnamon or vanilla extract (optional), for flavor

## INSTRUCTIONS:

1. Rinse the buckwheat under cold water and soak the raisins in warm water for 15 minutes, then drain. Chop the strawberries into pieces.
2. Combine milk and water in a saucepan, bring to a boil, and add the rinsed buckwheat. Reduce the heat to low and simmer for about 15 minutes, stirring occasionally, until the vegetables are softened and the liquid has been absorbed.
3. Serve the cooked porridge in bowls topped with strawberries, raspberries, blueberries, and raisins. Garnish with cream, cinnamon, or vanilla extract (optional), and sweetener to taste.

## PER SERVING:

Calories: 220 kcal; Fats: 4g; Protein: 8g; Carbs: 36g; Sugar: 10g; Fiber: 5g

# SUNNY-SIDE UP EGGS WITH PUMPKIN

## INGREDIENTS:

- 4 large eggs
- 150 g (1 cup) diced pumpkin
- 150 g (1 cup) sliced mushrooms
- 30 ml (2 tablespoons) olive oil
- 1 g (1/4 teaspoon) salt
- 1 g (1/4 teaspoon) black pepper
- 1 g (1/4 teaspoon) paprika
- 75 g (1/2 cup) diced onion
- Fresh parsley, chopped (optional)

## INSTRUCTIONS:

1. Heat the olive oil in a frying pan. Add the diced pumpkin and cook for 5 minutes, stirring occasionally, until it softens.
2. Add the sliced mushrooms and diced onion, and cook for 3–4 minutes, until the mushrooms are soft and the onion is translucent.
3. Push the vegetables to the edges of the pan. Crack the eggs into the center, season with salt, pepper, and paprika, and cover.
4. Cook for 3–4 minutes, until the egg whites have thickened and set. Remove from heat, cover, and let stand for 1 minute. Garnish with parsley if desired, and serve warm.

**PER SERVING:**
Calories: 320 kcal; Fats: 22g; Protein: 16g; Carbs: 12g; Sugar: 5g; Fiber: 3g

2 Portion  Easy  10 min  15 min

4 Portion  Easy  10 min  15 min

# PANCAKES WITH SMOKED SALMON

## INGREDIENTS:

- 60 g (1/2 cup) oat flour
- 150 ml (2/3 cup) milk
- 60 g (2 large) eggs
- 20 g (1 tablespoon) olive oil
- 5 g (1 teaspoon) maple syrup
- 0.6 g (1/8 teaspoon) salt
- 150 g (5 ounces) cream cheese
- 30 g (1 cup) fresh spinach leaves
- 150 g (5 ounces) smoked salmon

## INSTRUCTIONS:

1. Preheat a non-stick skillet over medium heat.
2. In one bowl, mix oat flour and salt. In another bowl, whisk together the milk, eggs, olive oil, and maple syrup until smooth. Combine the two mixtures, stirring gently to prevent the formation of lumps.
3. Pour 60 ml (1/4 cup) of batter onto the skillet, tilting it to spread the batter evenly. Cook the pancakes until bubbles form on the surface and the edges are set. Flip and cook for an additional 1–2 minutes, until golden brown on both sides. Repeat until all the batter is used.
4. Spread cream cheese on pancakes, layer with spinach leaves, and top with salmon. Fold into quarters or roll neatly. Serve warm.

**PER SERVING:**
Calories: 360 kcal; Fats: 22g; Protein: 32g; Carbs: 18g; Sugar: 10g; Fiber: 5g

# SAVORY MUSHROOM OATMEAL WITH POACHED EGGS

**2 Portion   Medium   5 min   20 min**

## INGREDIENTS:

- 90 g (1 cup) slow-cooking oatmeal
- 500 ml (2 cups) water
- 1 g (1/4 teaspoon) salt
- 15 ml (1 tablespoon) olive oil
- 150 g (1 cup) mushrooms, sliced

- 2 garlic cloves, minced
- 2 large eggs
- 15 ml (1 tablespoon) white vinegar
- Fresh herbs, chopped (for garnish)
- Salt and pepper, to taste

## INSTRUCTIONS:

1. Bring a saucepan of water and a pinch of salt to the boil. Add the oats and stir, being careful not to let them stick. Reduce the heat to low and simmer for 10-15 minutes, stirring occasionally, until the oats are creamy and fluffy.
2. While the oats are cooking, heat the olive oil in a frying pan over medium heat. Add the sliced mushrooms and fry for 5-7 minutes, stirring occasionally, until they are golden brown and fragrant. Add the crushed garlic to the pan and cook for an additional minute, allowing the flavors to meld beautifully.
3. In another saucepan, bring the water to a gentle simmer, add the vinegar, and stir quickly to create a swirl. Carefully crack the eggs into the centre of the swirl, one at a time. Poach the eggs for 3-4 minutes, until the whites are set but the yolks are still soft and runny. Carefully remove the eggs from the water and drain thoroughly to remove excess liquid.
4. Serve the oatmeal in bowls, with sautéed mushrooms and poached eggs. Garnish with fresh arugula leaves, sesame seeds, and sprouted chickpeas. Season with salt and pepper.

**PER SERVING:**
Calories: 320 kcal; Fats: 14g; Protein: 14g; Carbs: 35g; Sugar: 2g; Fiber: 4g

# CHICKEN AND MUSHROOM OMELET

**2 Portion**  **Medium**  **10 min**  **15 min**

## INGREDIENTS:

- 90 g (1 cup) slow-cooking oatmeal
- 500 ml (2 cups) water
- 1 g (1/4 teaspoon) salt
- 15 ml (1 tablespoon) olive oil
- 150 g (1 cup) cooked chicken, diced
- 150 g (1 cup) mushrooms, sliced
- 75 g (1/2 cup) onion, diced

- 4 large eggs
- 4 g (1 teaspoon) garlic powder
- 4 g (1 teaspoon) paprika
- 30 ml (2 tablespoons) milk
- Fresh parsley (for garnish)
- Salt and pepper, to taste

## INSTRUCTIONS:

1. Heat olive oil in a frying pan over medium heat. Sauté the diced onion for 2–3 minutes, until it is soft and fragrant. Add the mushrooms and cook for 5 minutes, stirring occasionally, until they release their juices and become tender.
2. Stir in the diced chicken and season with garlic powder, paprika, salt, and pepper. Cook for another 2 minutes, then remove from the heat and set aside.
3. In a bowl, whisk together the eggs, milk, salt, and pepper. Heat olive oil in another pan over medium heat. Pour the egg mixture into the pan and cook for 3–4 minutes until set but still slightly moist on top.
4. Place the chicken and mushroom mixture on one side of the omelet. Fold the other side over the filling and cook for 1 more minute. Transfer to a plate, garnish with parsley, and serve warm.

**PER SERVING:**
Calories: 350 kcal; Fats: 18g; Protein: 26g; Carbs: 10g; Sugar: 3g; Fiber: 1g

# OATMEAL WITH APPLES AND PECANS

## INGREDIENTS:

- 1 cup (90 g) rolled oats
- 120 ml (1/2 cup) water
- 120 ml (1/2 cup) almond milk
- 1 apple, peeled and sliced
- 1 tablespoon (10 g) dried cranberries (unsweetened)
- 2 tablespoons (20 g) pecans
- 1 tablespoon (15 ml) coconut oil
- 1/2 teaspoon (1.2 g) ground cinnamon
- Sweetener, to taste
- Pinch of salt

## INSTRUCTIONS:

1. Combine oats, water, almond milk, and salt in a saucepan. Bring to a boil, then reduce heat to low. Simmer for 5–7 minutes, stirring occasionally, until the oatmeal becomes soft and creamy.
2. While the oats are cooking, heat the coconut oil in a skillet. Add apple slices and sprinkle with cinnamon. Cook for 3-5 minutes, stirring, until the apples are softened and lightly caramelized.
3. Divide the cooked oatmeal into bowls, garnishing each with apples, pecans, and cranberries. Add sweetener if desired, and serve warm.

### PER SERVING:

Calories: 320 kcal; Fats: 14g; Protein: 6g; Carbs: 46g; Sugar: 15g; Fiber: 7g

2 Portion  Medium  5 min  20 min

# PUMPKIN RICE PORRIDGE

2 Portion  Medium  15 min  30 min

## INGREDIENTS:

- 90 g (1/2 cup) rice
- 150 g (1 cup) pumpkin, diced
- 120 ml (1/2 cup) milk (or almond milk)
- 2 g (1/2 teaspoon) ground cinnamon
- 360 ml (1 1/2 cups) water
- 1 g (1/4 teaspoon) ground nutmeg
- 1 g (1/4 teaspoon) ground ginger
- 15 ml (1 tablespoon) honey
- 15 ml (1 tablespoon) cream (10%)

## INSTRUCTIONS:

1. Preheat the oven to 200°C. Cut the pumpkin into cubes, place them on a parchment-lined baking sheet, and bake for 20 minutes or until soft. Rinse the rice under cold water. Cook it in a saucepan with water for 10 minutes or until tender.
2. Transfer the baked pumpkin into a saucepan to make a smooth puree. Add the cooked rice, milk, cinnamon, nutmeg, ginger, and cream. Stir well and cook over medium heat for 5 minutes, stirring occasionally.
3. Remove from heat, stir in the honey, and serve the porridge warm.

### PER SERVING:

Calories: 200 kcal; Fats: 4g; Protein: 5g; Carbs: 35g; Sugar: 12g; Fiber: 2g

# QUICHE WITH CHICKEN

## INGREDIENTS:

- 150 g (1 1/4 cups) whole wheat flour
- 75 g (1/3 cup) cold canola oil
- 2–3 tablespoons ice-cold water
- 60 g (1/2 cup) carrots, diced
- 1/4 teaspoon salt (for dough)
- 340 g (12 ounces) chicken breast
- 100 g (1 cup) broccoli florets
- 1 tablespoon black olives, sliced
- 75 g (1/2 cup) cherry tomatoes
- 5 large eggs
- 240 ml (1 cup) milk
- 60 g (1/4 cup) cheese mozzarella
- A pinch of salt and pepper

## INSTRUCTIONS:

1. Mix whole wheat flour with salt, then add vegetable oil to form crumbs. Next, mix in ice water to create the dough. Chill, roll out and pre-bake in a pie tin.
2. Whisk eggs with milk, salt, and spices. Layer the chicken vegetables, and olives on the crust, then pour the egg mixture over them. Sprinkle with cheese and bake until golden.
3. Let cool slightly and can be served warm or chilled.

### PER SERVING:

Calories: 342 kcal; Fats: 15g; Protein: 34g; Carbs: 22g; Sugar: 3g; Fiber: 3g

6 Portion  Medium  30 min  35 min

2 Portion  Medium  15 min  10 min

# LAZY COTTAGE CHEESE DUMPLINGS

## INGREDIENTS:

- 240 g (1 cup) cottage cheese, pressed or well-drained
- 60 g (1/4 cup) whole wheat flour (plus extra for dusting)
- 4 g (1 teaspoon) sugar substitute (optional)
- 1 large egg
- A pinch of salt
- 5 fresh raspberries
- 10 fresh blueberries
- Sour cream, for serving (optional)

## INSTRUCTIONS:

1. In a bowl, combine the cottage cheese, egg, whole wheat flour sugar substitute (if using), and a pinch of salt. Knead into a soft slightly sticky dough. Sprinkle the surface with flour and divide into 2-3 parts, forming strands 2-3 cm in diameter. Then cut into small pieces.
2. Bring a pan of salted water to a boil. Carefully add the vareniki to the water and cook for 2-3 minutes or until they float to the surface. Remove the vareniki with a slotted spoon.
3. Arrange on a serving plate, garnish with raspberries and blueberries and serve warm. Add sour cream to taste, if desired.

### PER SERVING:

Calories: 230 kcal; Fats: 8g; Protein: 16g; Carbs: 20g; Sugar: 4g; Fiber: 2g

# EGGS WITH ASPARAGUS AND SALMON

**2 Portion**   **Easy**   **5 min**   **10 min**

## INGREDIENTS:

- 4 large eggs
- 15 ml (1 tablespoon) milk or cream
- 2 ml (1/2 teaspoon) olive oil
- 8 asparagus spears, trimmed
- 113 g (4 ounces) smoked salmon, sliced

- 6 cherry tomatoes, halved
- Fresh basil leaves (for garnish)
- Salt and freshly ground black pepper, to taste

## INSTRUCTIONS:

1. Whisk the eggs with the milk, a pinch of salt, and freshly ground black pepper until well combined and slightly foamy.
2. Heat a non-stick frying pan over medium heat. Pour the egg mixture into the pan, allowing it to spread gently. Simmer the eggs, stirring occasionally with a spatula, until soft curds form and the eggs reach a delicate, creamy texture.
3. While the eggs are cooking, prepare the asparagus. Blanch the stalks in boiling water for 2 minutes, until they are slightly softened, retaining their vibrant color and crispness. Drain the asparagus and immediately transfer to a frying pan with heated olive oil. Lightly fry for 2 to 3 minutes over medium heat, stirring frequently, until softened and fragrant.
4. Carefully transfer the fried asparagus to a serving platter as a base. Spoon creamy scrambled eggs over the asparagus to create a rich and attractive layer. Top with smoked salmon slices and halved cherry tomatoes.
5. Garnish with fresh basil leaves. Serve warm.

### PER SERVING:
Calories: 220 kcal; Fats: 14 g; Protein: 18 g; Carbs: 4 g; Sugar: 2 g; Fiber: 2 g

# PINK PANCAKES WITH STRAWBERRIES

## INGREDIENTS:

- 1 1/2 cups (180 g) whole wheat flour
- 1/2 cup (60 g) almond flour
- 1 1/2 tablespoons (15 g) sugar substitute
- 1 1/2 teaspoons (6 g) baking powder
- 1/2 teaspoon (3 g) salt
- 1 cup (240 ml) nonfat Greek yogurt + 4 tablespoons (for serving)
- 2/3 cup (160 ml) beet puree
- 1 large egg
- 8 fresh strawberries, sliced

## INSTRUCTIONS:

1. In a bowl, combine whole wheat flour, almond flour, sugar substitute, baking powder and salt. Whisk the egg with the Greek yogurt and beetroot puree until smooth. Gently fold the dry ingredients into the liquid mixture, being careful not to overmix.
2. Heat the pan. Cook small batches of batter for 3 minutes until bubbles form, then flip and cook until done. Serve the pancakes warm, topped with strawberries and a dollop of Greek yogurt.

### PER SERVING:
Calories: 210 kcal; Fats: 5 g; Protein: 10 g; Carbs: 35 g; Sugar: 5 g; Fiber: 3 g

| 4 Portion | Easy | 10 min | 15 min |
| --- | --- | --- | --- |
| 2 Portion | Easy | 10 min | 20 min |

# BELGIAN COTTAGE CHEESE WAFFLES

## INGREDIENTS:

- 3 large eggs
- 1/2 cup (100 ml) almond milk
- 1 1/4 cups (300 g) cottage cheese
- 1 teaspoon baking powder
- A pinch of salt
- 1 cup (120 g) rice or oat flour

## INSTRUCTIONS:

1. Preheat the waffle iron and lightly grease it if necessary.
2. Combine the cottage cheese and eggs in a mixing bowl. Using a whisk or blender, beat the mixture until smooth and lump-free.
3. Then add the almond milk, flour, baking powder, and a pinch of salt. Mix thoroughly until the batter is smooth and lump-free.
4. Pour the batter into the waffle iron, spreading it out evenly. Close the waffle iron and cook for 4-5 minutes, or until the waffles are golden and crispy.
5. Serve warm with your favorite toppings, such as yogurt, fresh fruit, or honey.

### PER SERVING:
Calories: 220 kcal; Fats: 8 g; Protein: 12 g; Carbs: 20 g; Sugar: 2 g; Fiber: 2 g

# CHAPTER 3    SALADS

# SALAD WITH GOAT CHEESE, GRAPES, AND WALNUTS

**2 Portion**   **Easy**   **5 min**   **0 min**

## INGREDIENTS:

- 150 g (5 1/3 oz) mixed salad greens
- 120 g (4 1/4 oz) grapes
- 100 g (3 1/2 oz) goat cheese
- 60 g (2 oz) walnuts
- 30 ml (2 tablespoons) olive oil

- 15 ml (1 tablespoon) balsamic vinegar
- 7 g (1 teaspoon) honey (optional)
- Salt and black pepper, to taste

## INSTRUCTIONS:

1. Wash and dry the mixed greens thoroughly to keep them crisp and fresh. Place them in a large salad bowl, distributing them evenly to create a light, airy base for the other ingredients.
2. Next, prepare the grapes by halving them. Carefully slice the goat cheese. Chop the walnuts into smaller pieces to improve their texture and provide a delicious crunch.
3. Add the grape halves, goat cheese, and walnuts to the bowl with the greens, gently tossing them together.
4. Make the dressing in a separate small bowl by whisking the olive oil, balsamic vinegar, honey (if using), and a pinch of salt and freshly ground black pepper. Whisk until the ingredients are well combined, creating a smooth and flavorful dressing that complements the sweetness of the grapes and the richness of the cheese.
5. Drizzle the dressing evenly over the salad, making sure all ingredients are lightly coated. Use salad tongs to toss the mixture gently. Serve immediately.

— PER SERVING: —
Calories: 280 kcal; Fats: 20 g; Protein: 10 g; Carbs: 15 g; Sugar: 8 g; Fiber: 4 g

# PURPLE CAULIFLOWER SALAD

## INGREDIENTS:

- 140 g (5 oz) chicken breasts
- 150 g (1 cup) purple cauliflower
- 100 g (1 cup) broccoli
- 1/2 cucumber
- 1/2 red onion
- 60 g (1/2 cup) radicchio
- 30 g (1 cup) fresh spinach
- 30 g (2 tablespoons) walnuts
- 15 ml (1 tablespoon) olive oil
- 15 ml (1 tablespoon) lemon juice
- 5 g (1 teaspoon) Dijon mustard
- Salt and black pepper, to taste

## INSTRUCTIONS:

1. Season the chicken breasts with salt and black pepper, then fry them in a non-stick pan until they are done. Once cool, cut into pieces.
2. Separate the purple cauliflower and broccoli into florets and steam for 2-3 minutes, or until tender. Slice the cucumber, cut the red onion into thin half-moons, and cut the radicchio into large chunks.
3. Combine chopped vegetables and chicken. Top with walnuts.
4. Whisk together the olive oil, lemon juice, Dijon mustard, salt, and black pepper, then pour over the salad and toss. Serve immediately.

### PER SERVING:
Calories: 320 kcal; Fats: 18 g; Protein: 28 g; Carbs: 12 g; Sugar: 5 g; Fiber: 4 g

# SALMON SALAD WITH PINEAPPLE

## INGREDIENTS:

- 200 g (7 oz) salmon fillets
- 150 g (2 cups) salad greens
- 60 g (2.1 oz) sliced almonds
- 120 g (1/2 cup) pineapple, peeled and chopped
- 1 garlic clove
- 30 ml (2 tablespoons) olive oil
- 5 ml (1 teaspoon) Dijon mustard
- 15 ml (1 tablespoon) lemon juice
- Salt and black pepper, to taste

## INSTRUCTIONS:

1. Pat the salmon fillets dry, check for bones, and remove any that are found. Season with salt and black pepper, then let them sit for 10 minutes. Heat 15 ml (1 tablespoon) of olive oil in a frying pan. Fry the salmon for 5 minutes on each side, turning it once. Leave to cool slightly, then cut into pieces.
2. Cut the pineapple into small pieces. Crush the garlic. In a bowl, combine the salad greens, pineapple, and almonds. Add the salmon pieces. Whisk together the remaining olive oil, lemon juice, Dijon mustard, minced garlic, salt, and black pepper in a separate bowl.
3. Drizzle the dressing over the salad, toss gently to coat, and serve immediately.

### PER SERVING:
Calories: 340 kcal; Fats: 22 g; Protein: 30 g; Carbs: 15 g; Sugar: 9 g; Fiber: 3 g

2 Portion    Easy    10 min    10 min

# SALAD WITH AVOCADO AND FETA

## INGREDIENTS:

- 100 g (1/2 medium) avocado
- 80 g (1/2 cup) feta cheese
- 50 g (1 small) red onion
- 120 g (4 cups) mixed leafy greens
- 10 g (2 teaspoons) sesame seeds
- 150 g (1 medium) cucumber
- 20 g (2 tablespoons) chopped walnuts
- 15 ml (1 tablespoon) olive oil
- 10 ml (2 teaspoons) lemon juice
- A pinch of salt
- A pinch of black pepper

## INSTRUCTIONS:

1. Thinly slice the red onion, cucumber, and avocado.
2. Combine the mixed leafy greens, avocado slices, cucumber, red onion, and chopped walnuts in a large bowl.
3. Add the cubed feta cheese and sprinkle with sesame seeds.
4. Whisk together olive oil, lemon juice, salt, and black pepper to prepare the dressing. Drizzle the dressing over the salad and toss gently. Serve immediately.

### PER SERVING:
Calories: 210 kcal; Fats: 15 g; Protein: 5 g; Carbs: 12 g; Sugars: 4 g; Fiber: 4 g

2 Portion    Easy    10 min    0 min

2 Portion    Easy    10 min    5 min

# SHRIMPS SALAD WITH MANGO

## INGREDIENTS:

- 200 g (7 ounces) cooked and peeled shrimp
- 100 g (3.5 ounces) cherry tomatoes, halved
- 200 g (7 ounces) avocado, diced
- 100 g (3.5 ounces) mixed salad greens
- 150 g (5.3 ounces) ripe mango, diced
- 30 ml (2 tablespoons) olive oil
- 15 ml (1 tablespoon) lemon juice
- 1 teaspoon honey (optional)
- Salt and pepper to taste

## INSTRUCTIONS:

1. Combine the mixed greens, halved cherry tomatoes, diced avocado, and mango pieces in a large bowl.
2. Heat 1 tablespoon of olive oil in a skillet over medium heat. Sauté the shrimp for 2–3 minutes, until they are lightly golden.
3. In a small bowl, whisk the remaining olive oil, lemon juice, honey (if using), salt, and pepper until the dressing is smooth.
4. Add the warm shrimp to the salad, drizzle with the dressing, and gently toss everything together. Serve immediately for a fresh and flavorful meal.

### PER SERVING:
Calories: 310 kcal; Fats: 22g; Protein: 9g; Carbs: 20g; Sugar: 10g; Fiber: 6g

# CHICKPEA AND SPINACH SALAD WITH BROCCOLI

**2 Portion   Medium   15 min   90 min**

## INGREDIENTS:

- 200 g (1 cup) chickpeas (preferably cooked)
- 120 g (approximately 4 loosely packed cups) fresh spinach
- 100 g (1 cup) broccoli florets
- 1 red bell pepper (approx. 100 g)
- 50 g (1/3 cup) pitted olives
- 1 medium zucchini (approx. 150 g)
- For the Dressing:
- 15 ml (1 tablespoon) olive oil
- 15 ml (1 tablespoon) lemon juice
- 1 garlic clove, minced
- Salt and black pepper, to taste

## INSTRUCTIONS:

1. Soak the chickpeas overnight and cook them in fresh water until tender (about 60 minutes). Then, drain and set aside.
2. Cook the broccoli florets in boiling water for 2-3 minutes, until they are soft. Then, drain and let them cool. Place the red pepper on a chopping board, remove the core and seeds, and slice it thinly. Halve the pitted olives.
3. Brush the zucchini with olive oil, then slice it into thin slices. Grill them in a preheated grill pan over medium heat for about 3-4 minutes on each side, until they have grill marks; then slice or break them into bite-sized strips.
4. Combine chickpeas, fresh spinach, steamed broccoli, sliced red bell pepper, olive halves, and grilled zucchini pieces in a large bowl. Whisk together olive oil, lemon juice, minced garlic, salt, and black pepper in a small bowl until smooth.
5. Drizzle dressing over salad, tossing gently. Serve immediately.

— PER SERVING: —
Calories: 280 kcal; Fats: 12 g; Protein: 10 g; Carbs: 32 g; Sugar: 6 g; Fiber: 8 g

# SALAD WITH FETA AND PERSIMMON

## INGREDIENTS:

- 100 g (1/2 persimmon)
- 15 g (1/8 cup) pomegranate seeds
- 113 g (4 oz) low-fat feta cheese
- 60 g (2 cups) fresh mixed greens
- 7 g (1/2 tablespoon) olive oil
- 15 g (1 tablespoon) pistachio
- 15 ml (1 tablespoon) lemon juice
- 7 g (1 teaspoon) honey
- Salt and black pepper, to tast

## INSTRUCTIONS:

1. Wash the persimmons and slice them into even rings. Set aside.
2. Arrange the mixed greens on a serving platter, spreading then evenly to create a base. Then layer the persimmon rings pomegranate seeds, diced feta cheese, and pistachios.
3. Whisk together the olive oil, lemon juice, honey, salt, and blac pepper in a small bowl until the dressing is fully emulsified.
4. Drizzle the dressing evenly over the salad, ensuring all ingredient are thinly coated. Toss gently. Serve the salad immediately.

### PER SERVING:

Calories: 280 kcal; Fats: 16g; Protein: 12g; Carbs: 18g; Sugar: 10g; Fiber: 4g

| 2 Portion | Easy | 5 min | 0 min |
| 4 Portion | Easy | 10 min | 0 min |

# TUNA AND VEGETABLE SALAD

## INGREDIENTS:

- 1 can of canned tuna, drained
- 2 medium cucumbers, sliced into rounds
- 1/2 cup (80 g) corn
- 1/3 cup (50 g) pitted olives, whole
- 1/2 red onion, thinly sliced into half-moons
- 2 cups (100 g) mixed salad greens
- 2 tablespoons (30 ml) olive o
- 1 tablespoon (15 ml) lemon juice
- Lemon wedges for garnish
- Salt and black pepper, to tast

## INSTRUCTIONS:

1. Slice the cucumbers into rounds and the red onion into thin hal moons.
2. Combine the green salads, cucumber slices, corn, red onion, an canned tuna in a large bowl, keeping the tuna in chunks. Add th whole olives to the mix.
3. Drizzle the salad with olive oil and lemon juice. Season with salt an black pepper to taste. Toss will coat all ingredients evenly with th dressing. Garnish the salad with lemon wedges before serving.
4. Garnish the salad with lemon wedges before serving.

### PER SERVING:

Calories: 150 kcal; Fats: 7 g; Protein: 12 g; Carbs: 10 g; Sugar: 3 g; Fiber: 2 g

# RED CABBAGE SALAD WITH SESAME

**2 Portion**   **Easy**   **10 min**   **0 min**

## INGREDIENTS:

- 200 g (2 cups) red cabbage
- 100 g (1 medium) carrot
- 100 g (1 medium) bell pepper
- 15 g (1/4 cup) fresh parsley
- 10 g (1 tablespoon) sesame seeds
- 30 g (2 tablespoons) peanut butter
- 15 ml (1 tablespoon) soy sauce

- 15 ml (1 tablespoon) lemon juice
- 5 ml (1 teaspoon) sesame oil
- 1 garlic clove, minced
- 15 ml (1 tablespoon) water (to adjust consistency)
- Salt and black pepper, to taste

## INSTRUCTIONS:

1. Thinly shred the red cabbage, sprinkle it with salt, and gently massage it with your hands for about 1 minute, until it softens and releases its juices.
2. Slice the carrot and bell pepper into thin strips, then add them to the cabbage. Toss everything together. Chop the parsley and mix it with the vegetables along with sesame seeds, ensuring they are well incorporated.
3. To prepare the dressing, whisk together peanut butter, soy sauce, lemon juice, sesame oil, minced garlic, and water until smooth. Add more water to achieve the desired consistency if the dressing is too thick. Adjust salt and pepper to taste.
4. Drizzle the dressing over the salad, and sit for 5 minutes to absorb the flavors. Serve fresh, garnished with additional sesame seeds if desired.

**PER SERVING:**
Calories: 240 kcal; Fats: 13 g; Protein: 8 g; Carbs: 18 g; Sugar: 8 g; Fiber: 5 g

# SALAD WITH BAKED EGGPLANT

## INGREDIENTS:

- 250 g (1 medium) eggplant
- 150 g (1 cup) cherry tomatoes
- 30 ml (2 tablespoons) olive oil
- 10 g (1/4 cup) fresh basil leaves
- 15 ml (1 tablespoon) balsamic vinegar
- 80 g (1/2 cup) feta cheese
- Salt and black pepper, to taste

## INSTRUCTIONS:

1. Preheat the oven to 400°F (200°C). Cut the eggplant into 1.25 cm x 1.25 cm (1/2 inch x 1/2 inch) squares and brush them with olive oil. Arrange the cubes on a parchment-lined baking sheet.
2. Bake for 10 to 15 minutes, until eggplant is soft and golden brown. Let cool slightly.
3. Combine roasted eggplant, cherry tomato halves, and fresh basil leaves in a large salad bowl. Whisk olive oil, balsamic vinegar, salt, and pepper in a small bowl to create dressing. Drizzle over salad and toss gently.
4. Top with diced feta cheese and serve immediately.

### PER SERVING:
Calories: 220 kcal; Fats: 14g; Protein: 7g; Carbs: 16g; Sugars: 8g; Fiber: 5g

**2 Portion**   **Easy**   **10 min**   **15 min**

**2 Portion**   **Easy**   **10 min**   **20 min**

# LENTIL SALAD WITH MIX VEGETABLES

## INGREDIENTS:

- 120 g (3/4 cup) dry lentils
- 150 g (1 medium) bell pepper
- 150 g (1 medium) tomato
- 50 g (1/3 cup) black olives
- 150 g (1 medium) cucumber
- 50 g (1 small) red onion
- 15 ml (1 tablespoon) olive oil
- 10 ml (2 teaspoons) lemon juice
- Salt and black pepper, to taste

## INSTRUCTIONS:

1. Cook the lentils in boiling water for 20 minutes or until tender. Drain and let them cool.
2. Dice the bell pepper and tomato. Slice the cucumber into half-moons and the red onion into thin strips.
3. Combine the cooked lentils, diced vegetables, and black olives in a large salad bowl.
4. Whisk together olive oil, lemon juice, salt, and black pepper to make the dressing. Pour over the salad and toss gently to combine.
5. Serve immediately or let it chill for 10–15 minutes for the flavors to blend.

### PER SERVING:
Calories: 220 kcal; Fats: 6g; Protein: 10g; Carbs: 32g; Sugars: 6g; Fiber: 9g

# CHAPTER 4 — SOUPS

# SOUP WITH VEGETABLES AND CHICKEN

**4 Portion**  **Easy**  **15 min**  **35 min**

## INGREDIENTS:

- 10.5 oz (300 g) chicken fillet
- 1 bell pepper, diced
- 2 medium potatoes, diced
- 1 carrot, grated or diced
- 5.3 oz (150 g) champignon mushrooms, sliced

- 1 onion, finely chopped
- 1 tablespoon (15 ml) vegetable oil
- 6 1/3 cups (1.5 liters) water or chicken broth
- Salt and pepper, to taste
- Chopped green onions, for garnish

## INSTRUCTIONS:

1. Heat vegetable oil in a pot over medium heat. Add the chopped onion and sauté for 2 minutes until translucent.
2. Add the carrot and mushrooms, stirring occasionally, and cook for 5 minutes.
3. Pour water or chicken broth into the pot, ensuring the liquid fully covers the vegetables. Add the diced chicken fillet and bring to a boil. While boiling, skim off any foam on the surface to maintain a clear and appetizing broth. Reduce the heat to a gentle simmer and let the chicken cook for 10 minutes, allowing the flavors to meld together.
4. Add diced potatoes and bell pepper. Season with salt and pepper, and cook for 15 minutes until the potatoes are tender.
5. Taste and adjust the seasoning if needed. Serve the soup hot, garnished with chopped green onions.

**PER SERVING:**
Calories: 120 kcal; Fats: 4 g; Protein: 12 g; Carbs: 10 g; Sugar: 3 g; Fiber: 2 g

# YELLOW TOMATO GAZPACHO

## INGREDIENTS:

- 600 g (1.3 lb) yellow tomatoes
- 10.5 ounces (300 g) chicken breast
- 1 yellow bell pepper, chopped
- 1 small cucumber, chopped
- 1 garlic clove, minced
- 2 tablespoons olive oil
- 1 tablespoon white wine vinegar
- Salt and pepper, to taste
- Fresh basil or parsley (for garnish)

## INSTRUCTIONS:

1. Boil the chicken until done (about 12-15 minutes). Cool slightly.
2. Place the chopped tomatoes, pepper, cucumber, garlic, and cooked chicken in a blender or food processor. Blend until smooth. Add olive oil, vinegar, salt, and pepper. Blend again until completely combined. Refrigerate for 2 hours to allow the flavors to develop.
3. Mix thoroughly, then pour into bowls and garnish with fresh basil or parsley, sliced cherry tomatoes, and diced cucumber. If desired, add a couple of slices of pepper.

### PER SERVING:

Calories: 250; Fats: 10 g; Protein: 25 g; Carbs: 12 g; Sugar: 5 g; Fiber: 3 g

**4 Portion** **Easy** **15 min** **5 min**

# SOUP WITH SPINACH AND MEATBALLS

**4 Portion** **Easy** **15 min** **25 min**

## INGREDIENTS:

- 1 large egg
- 1 garlic clove, minced
- 1/2 teaspoon (2 g) paprika
- Salt and pepper, to taste
- 1 onion, finely chopped
- 1 carrot, diced
- 2 medium potatoes, diced
- 1 tablespoon (15 ml) olive oil
- 10.5 ounces (300 g) ground beef
- 1 cup (30 g) fresh spinach leaves, chopped
- 6 1/3 cups (1.5 liters) water
- Fresh parsley or dill, chopped (for garnish)

## INSTRUCTIONS:

1. Combine the minced meat, egg, crushed garlic, paprika, salt, and pepper in a bowl. Mix thoroughly, form into meatballs, and set aside. Heat the olive oil in a saucepan. Add the chopped onion and fry for 2 minutes until soft. Add the carrots and cook for 3 minutes.
2. Pour in the water and bring to a boil. Add the chopped potatoes and meatballs to the soup. Cook for 10 minutes, stirring occasionally, until the mixture is tender and the vegetables are cooked through. Add the chopped spinach and cook for another 2 minutes.
3. Taste and adjust the seasonings if necessary. Serve hot.

### PER SERVING:

Calories: 220 kcal; Fats: 10 g; Protein: 16 g; Carbs: 15 g; Sugar: 3 g; Fiber: 2 g

# CREAMY PUMPKIN SOUP

## INGREDIENTS:

- 500 g (1.1 lb) pumpkin, peeled and cubed
- 1 small onion, chopped
- 1 garlic clove, minced
- 2 tablespoons olive oil
- 500 ml (2 cups) vegetable broth
- 200 ml (¾ cup) unsweetened oat milk or almond milk
- ¼ teaspoon ground nutmeg
- Salt and pepper, to taste
- Pumpkin seeds and fresh herbs (for garnish)

## INSTRUCTIONS:

1. Heat the olive oil in a large saucepan over medium heat. Add the onion and garlic and cook for 3-4 minutes until softened.
2. Add the pumpkin cubes and cook for 5 minutes, stirring occasionally. Pour in the vegetable stock, bring to a boil, then reduce the heat and simmer for 15-20 minutes, until the pumpkin is tender. Remove from the heat, process until smooth, and stir in the oat or almond milk with nutmeg, salt, and pepper.
3. Serve, garnished with dry-fried onions, pumpkin seeds, and herbs.

### PER SERVING:
Calories: 160 kcal; Fats: 7g; Protein: 3g; Carbs: 20g; Sugar: 6g; Fiber: 4g

**4 Portion**   **Easy**   **10 min**   **25 min**

**2 Portion**   **Easy**   **5 min**   **6 min**

# BEAN SOUP WITH TOMATOES

## INGREDIENTS:

- 250 ml (1 cup) dried white beans, soaked overnight
- 500 ml (2 cups) fresh tomatoes
- 1 medium onion, finely chopped
- 2–3 cloves garlic, crushed
- 1 carrot, diced
- 1 stalk celery, diced
- 1 liter (4 cups) vegetable broth
- 2 tablespoons (30 ml) tomato paste
- Salt and black pepper to taste
- 1 tablespoon olive oil
- Fresh parsley, chopped (for garnish)

## INSTRUCTIONS:

1. Rinse the soaked white beans. Boil them in fresh water until tender, about 30 minutes. Drain and set aside.
2. Heat the olive oil in a large saucepan over medium heat. Sauté the chopped onion, carrot, and celery for 5 minutes. Add the crushed garlic and tomato paste to the pan. Stir and cook for 2 minutes. Add the peeled and chopped tomatoes, as well as the cooked beans.
3. Pour in the vegetable broth and bring the soup to a simmer. Reduce the heat and simmer for 15–20 minutes. Season with salt and black pepper to taste. Serve hot, garnished with fresh parsley.

### PER SERVING:
Calories: 180 kcal; Fats: 4 g; Protein: 8 g; Carbs: 28 g; Sugar: 6 g; Fiber: 6 g

# DELICIOUS RED LENTIL AND VEGETABLE SOUP

**4 Portion**  **Easy**  **15 min**  **40 min**

## INGREDIENTS:

- 15 g (1 tablespoon) olive oil
- 100 g (1 medium) onion, chopped
- 10 g (1 clove) garlic, minced
- 100 g (1 medium) carrot, diced
- 100 g (1/2 cup) red lentils, rinsed
- 1.5 g (1/2 teaspoon) ground coriander
- 1.5 g (1/2 teaspoon) smoked paprika

- 500 g (2 cups) chicken broth
- 200 g (7.25 oz) diced tomatoes
- 75 g (1/2 medium) potato, peeled and diced
- Salt and pepper, to taste
- 5 g (1 bunch) parsley, chopped (for garnish)

## INSTRUCTIONS:

1. Heat the olive oil in a large saucepan over medium heat. When the oil is hot, add the finely chopped onion and diced carrot, stirring frequently.
2. Sauté the vegetables for about 5 minutes, or until the onion is translucent and the carrots have softened. Add the crushed garlic to the pan. Then sprinkle the ground coriander and smoked paprika over the vegetables. Cook for 1–2 minutes to release the flavours. Add the red lentils to the pan, followed by the diced tomatoes and chicken stock. Stir the mixture and bring it to a gentle simmer.
3. Let the soup simmer for 15 minutes, stirring occasionally, until the lentils have softened but are not yet fully cooked. Add the diced potatoes to the pan, stirring to combine with the soup. Continue simmering for an additional 15 to 20 minutes, stirring occasionally, until the lentils and potatoes are tender and cooked through. Season the soup with salt and freshly ground black pepper to taste.
4. Serve the soup hot, ladle into bowls. Garnish generously with freshly chopped parsley.

**PER SERVING:**
Calories: 180 kcal; Fats: 6g; Protein: 7g; Carbs: 24g; Sugar: 5g; Fiber: 5g

# SALMON AND VEGETABLE SOUP

## INGREDIENTS:

- 10.5 ounces (300 g) salmon, cubed
- 2 medium potatoes, diced
- 1 carrot, sliced into rounds
- 1 onion, finely chopped
- 1 liter (4 cups) water or vegetabl broth
- Salt and pepper, to taste
- 1 tablespoon (15 ml) olive oil
- Fresh dill, chopped (for garnish)

## INSTRUCTIONS:

1. Heat olive oil in a large pot over medium heat. Add the choppe onion and sauté until soft and translucent, about 3 minutes.
2. Add the sliced carrot and diced potato to the pot. Pour in the wate or vegetable broth, bring to a boil, then reduce the heat to mediu and simmer for 15 minutes, or until the vegetables are tender.
3. Gently add the cubed salmon to the pot. Simmer for an addition 10 minutes, until the fish is fully cooked and flaky.
4. Season with salt and pepper to taste.
5. Serve the soup hot, garnished with fresh dill for a burst of flavor.

### PER SERVING:
Calories: 220 kcal; Fats: 10g; Protein: 16g; Carbs: 10g; Sugar: 3g; Fiber: 2g

**4 Portion    Easy    10 min    30 min**

**2 Portion    Easy    5 min    6 min**

# BROCCOLI AND CAULIFLOWER SOUP

## INGREDIENTS:

- 2 medium potatoes, diced
- 1 carrot, sliced into rounds
- 1 onion, finely chopped
- 5.3 ounces (150 g) broccoli florets
- 5.3 ounces (150 g) cauliflower florets
- 1 zucchini, cut into wedges
- 4 cups (1 liter) vegetable broth or water
- Salt and pepper, to taste
- 1 tablespoon (15 ml) olive oi
- Basil sprig (for garnish)

## INSTRUCTIONS:

1. Heat olive oil in a large pot over medium heat. Sauté the choppe onion for about 3 minutes, until translucent.
2. Add the sliced carrot, diced potato, and zucchini wedges to the po Stir and cook for 5 minutes.
3. Pour in the vegetable broth or water, bring to a boil, then reduce th heat to medium and simmer for 15 minutes, or until the vegetable are tender. Add the broccoli florets and cauliflower florets to th soup. Cook for an additional 10 minutes, until the florets are tende yet still vibrant. Season the soup with salt and pepper to taste.
4. Serve hot, garnished with a sprig of basil for a fresh, aromatic touc

### PER SERVING:
Calories: 150 kcal; Fats: 3 g; Protein: 5 g; Carbs: 25 g; Sugar: 7 g; Fiber: 5 g

# CHAPTER 5

# FISH & SEAFOOD

# SALMON WITH LEMON SAUCE

**4 Portion**   **Medium**   **10 min**   **15 min**

## INGREDIENTS:

- 4 salmon fillets (600 g), skinless
- 1/2 cup (60 g) all-purpose flour
- 1 teaspoon (5 g) garlic powder
- 1 teaspoon (5 g) smoked paprika
- Salt and pepper, to taste
- 2 tablespoons (30 ml) olive oil
- 2 tablespoons (30 g) butter
- 1/4 cup (60 ml) fresh lemon juice
- 2 tablespoons (30 g) capers, drained
- 1/2 teaspoon (2 g) lemon zest
- 1/4 cup (60 ml) chicken or vegetable stock
- Fresh dill, for garnish

## INSTRUCTIONS:

1. Combine flour, garlic powder, smoked paprika, salt, and pepper in a shallow dish. Dredge each salmon fillet in the flour mixture, coating it evenly on all sides.
2. Heat olive oil in a skillet over medium-high heat. Add the salmon fillets and cook for 3–4 minutes per side, or until the exterior is crispy and golden brown on both sides.
3. After removing the salmon, reduce the heat to medium and add butter to the skillet. Once melted, stir in lemon juice, capers, lemon zest, and chicken or vegetable stock. Simmer for 2–3 minutes, allowing the sauce to thicken slightly. Adjust seasoning with salt and pepper if needed.
4. Plate the crispy salmon fillets and drizzle with the tangy lemon caper sauce directly from the skillet. Garnish with fresh dill for a fragrant and vibrant finish.

**PER SERVING:**
Calories: 350 kcal; Fats: 22 g; Protein: 25 g; Carbs: 12 g; Sugar: 1 g; Fiber: 0 g

# MUSSELS WITH LEMON AND PARSLEY

## INGREDIENTS:

- 2 lbs (900 g) mussels, cleaned and debearded
- 2 tablespoons (30 ml) olive oil
- 2 cloves (10 g) garlic, minced
- 1 cup (240 ml) white wine
- 1 lemon, zested and juiced
- 1/4 cup (15 g) fresh parsley, chopped
- 1/4 cup (15 g) fresh cilantro, chopped
- Salt and pepper, to taste
- Lemon wedges, for serving

## INSTRUCTIONS:

1. Heat the olive oil. Add minced garlic and cook for about 1 minute.
2. Pour in the white wine and bring to a boil. Reduce the heat to low and let it simmer for 2 minutes.
3. Add the mussels to the pot. Cover with a lid and cook for 5–7 minutes. Stir in lemon zest, lemon juice, chopped parsley, cilantro, salt, and pepper. Mix well. Remove the pot from the heat.
4. Serve the mussels hot in the sauce, garnished with fresh lemon wedges.

### PER SERVING:

Calories: 180 kcal; Fats: 8 g; Protein: 18 g; Carbs: 6 g; Sugar: 1 g; Fiber: 1 g

| 4 Portion | Easy | 10 min | 10 min |
| 2 Portion | Easy | 10 min | 7 min |

# SHRIMPS WITH LIME AND OREGANO

## INGREDIENTS:

- 1 lb (450 g) shrimp, peeled and deveined
- 2 tablespoons (30 ml) olive oil
- 1 tablespoon (15 g) fresh oregano (or 1 teaspoon dried oregano)
- Juice of 2 limes (about 60 ml)
- Zest of 1 lime
- 2 cloves (10 g) garlic, minced
- Salt and pepper, to taste
- Fresh cilantro or parsley, chopped (optional, for garnish)

## INSTRUCTIONS:

1. Heat olive oil in a large skillet over medium heat. Add minced garlic and sauté for about 30 seconds, until fragrant.
2. Add shrimp to the skillet. Sprinkle with oregano, salt, and pepper. Cook for 2–3 minutes per side, or until shrimp are pink and opaque.
3. Pour in lime juice and sprinkle with lime zest. Toss to coat the shrimp evenly, allowing the flavors to combine for 1–2 minutes.
4. Remove from heat and garnish with fresh cilantro or parsley, if desired. Serve hot with your favorite side dish, like rice or a fresh green salad.

### PER SERVING:

Calories: 180 kcal; Fats: 8 g; Protein: 24 g; Carbs: 2 g; Sugar: 0 g; Fiber: 0 g

# GRILLED SARDINES WITH ROSEMARY

## INGREDIENTS:

- 10–12 fresh sardines, cleaned
- 2 tablespoons (30 ml) extra virgin olive oil
- Juice of 1 lemon
- 1 teaspoon (5 g) dried oregano
- 1 teaspoon (5 g) dried thyme
- 2 cloves (10 g) garlic, minced
- Salt and pepper, to taste
- 2 teaspoons (2 g) fresh rosemary, chopped
- Lemon slices, for serving

## INSTRUCTIONS:

1. Preheat the grill. Rinse the sardines under cold water and pat d with paper towels.
2. Lightly brush each sardine with olive oil and season both sides wi salt, pepper, oregano, thyme, crushed garlic, and chopped rosemar Place the sardines on the hot grill. Cook for 3 to 4 minutes on ea side, or until the skin is crisp and the fish flakes easily with a fork.
3. Transfer the grilled sardines to a serving platter.
4. Serve hot, garnished with lemon wedges.

### PER SERVING:

Calories: 190 kcal; Fats: 12 g; Protein: 22 g; Carbs: 2 g; Sugar: 0 g; Fiber: 0 g

4 Portion  Medium  10 min  8 min

2 Portion  Medium  10 min  25 min

# BAKED SEA BREAM

## INGREDIENTS:

- 1 sea bream, cleaned and filleted (about 300 g)
- 2 tablespoons (30 ml) olive oil
- Juice of 1 lemon (30 ml)
- 2 cloves (10 g) garlic, minced
- 1 teaspoon (5 g) dried thyme
- Salt, to taste
- Pepper mix, to taste
- Salad mix (arugula, spinach, lettuce), for serving

## INSTRUCTIONS:

1. Preheat the oven to 375°F (190°C). Line a baking tray wi parchment paper.
2. Rinse the sea bream fillets under cold water and pat dry with pap towels. In a small bowl, combine olive oil, lemon juice, minc garlic, dried thyme, salt, and pepper. Brush the fillets generous with this mixture, ensuring even coverage.
3. Arrange the sea bream fillets on the prepared baking tray. Bake the preheated oven for 20–25 minutes, or until the fish is ful cooked and flakes easily with a fork.
4. Serve the oven-baked sea bream hot, accompanied by a fresh sal mix for a healthy and vibrant meal.

### PER SERVING:

Calories: 260 kcal; Fats: 14 g; Protein: 26 g; Carbs: 4 g; Sugar: 1 g; Fiber: 1 g

# GRILLED MACKEREL

**2 Portion**  **Easy**  **10 min**  **10 min**

## INGREDIENTS:

- 2 fresh mackerels, cleaned and gutted (about 600 g)
- 2 tablespoons (30 ml) extra virgin olive oil
- Salt and pepper, to taste
- 1 lemon, sliced into rings
- A few sprigs of fresh dill (optional, for garnish)

## INSTRUCTIONS:

1. Preheat your grill to medium-high heat, ensuring it reaches the proper temperature for even cooking.
2. Rinse the mackerels thoroughly under cold running water to remove any impurities, and pat them dry using paper towels. This step ensures the skin crisps up beautifully while grilling.
3. Using a brush, coat each fish generously with olive oil on both sides to prevent sticking and add a touch of richness. Season the mackerels evenly with salt and freshly ground black pepper to enhance their natural flavors.
4. Prepare the fish for grilling by placing several thin slices of fresh lemon inside each cavity. This infuses the mackerel with a subtle citrus aroma as it cooks. Place the prepared fish on the grill grate and cook for 7–8 minutes on each side, turning once. The skin should turn golden and crispy, while the flesh becomes tender and flakes easily with a fork. Be careful not to overcook, as this may dry out the fish.
5. Once the mackerel is grilled to perfection, carefully transfer it to a serving plate. Garnish each fish with a sprig of fresh dill and additional lemon slices, if desired.
6. Serve hot and savor this delightful, tangy dish.

---
**PER SERVING:**
Calories: 290 kcal; Fats: 18 g; Protein: 28 g; Carbs: 2 g; Sugar: 0 g; Fiber: 0 g

# FRIED COD WITH ASPARAGUS

**4 Portion**  **Medium**  **10 min**  **15 min**

## INGREDIENTS:

- 4 cod fillets (600 g), skinless
- 1/2 cup (60 g) all-purpose flour
- 1 teaspoon (5 g) garlic powder
- 1 teaspoon (5 g) paprika
- Salt and pepper, to taste
- 3 tablespoons (45 ml) olive oil, for frying
- 1 lb (450 g) fresh asparagus, trimmed
- 1 tablespoon (15 ml) olive oil
- 2 cloves (10 g) garlic, minced
- Zest of 1 lemon
- Salt and pepper, to taste

## INSTRUCTIONS:

1. Prepare the cod: In a shallow dish, mix flour, garlic powder, paprika, salt, and pepper.
2. Pat the cod fillets dry with paper towels and dredge them in the flour mixture, ensuring an even coating on all sides.
3. Heat olive oil in a skillet over medium heat. Fry the fillets for 3–4 minutes per side, or until golden brown and cooked through. Transfer to a plate lined with paper towels to remove excess oil.
4. In the same skillet, heat 1 tablespoon of olive oil over medium heat. Add the minced garlic and sauté for 30 seconds until fragrant. Toss the asparagus in the skillet, season with salt and pepper, and cook for 5–7 minutes, stirring occasionally, until tender and crisp.
5. Add the lemon zest and stir to combine for a burst of flavor. Plate the fried cod alongside the sautéed asparagus. Garnish with additional lemon zest or fresh parsley for an extra burst of freshness. Enjoy immediately!

**PER SERVING:**
Calories: 290 kcal; Fats: 14 g; Protein: 25 g; Carbs: 9 g; Sugar: 2 g; Fiber: 2 g

# GRILLED COD FILLET

## INGREDIENTS:

- 4 cod fillets (600 g), skinless
- 2 tablespoons (30 ml) olive oil
- 1 teaspoon (5 g) garlic powder
- 1 teaspoon (5 g) paprika
- Salt and pepper, to taste
- 1 cup (150 g) baby carrots
- 1 cup (150 g) Brussels sprouts
- 1 cup (150 g) broccoli florets
- 1 cup (150 g) cauliflower florets
- 1 1/2 cups (200 g) corn salad
- Juice of 1 lime (15 ml)
- 1 tablespoon (15 ml) olive oil

## INSTRUCTIONS:

1. Preheat the grill. Brush the cod fillets with olive oil and season with garlic powder, paprika, salt, and pepper. Grill the fillets on each side for 4-5 minutes, until golden brown.
2. Combine the baby carrots, Brussels sprouts, broccoli, and cauliflower in a steamer. Steam for 5-7 minutes, until tender but slightly crisp.
3. Place the Corn Salad and cooked vegetables on a plate.
4. Top with the cod fillets. Serve warm.

### PER SERVING:
Calories: 305 kcal; Fats: 12 g; Protein: 27 g; Carbs: 18 g; Sugar: 5 g; Fiber: 3 g

| 4 Portion | Easy | 15 min | 20 min |
| --- | --- | --- | --- |
| 2 Portion | Easy | 10 min | 10 min |

# GRILLED FISH IN TOMATO SAUCE

## INGREDIENTS:

- 4 fillets of white fish (e.g., cod, haddock, or tilapia)
- 2 tablespoons (30 ml) olive oil
- Salt and pepper, to taste
- 2 cups (480 ml) tomato purée
- 1 teaspoon (5 g) sugar (optional, to balance acidity)
- 2 cloves (10 g) garlic, minced
- 1/2 teaspoon (2 g) dried oregano
- 1/2 teaspoon (2 g) dried thyme
- 1/4 teaspoon (1 g) chili flakes (optional, for heat)
- 1/4 cup (15 g) fresh basil leaves, chopped

## INSTRUCTIONS:

1. Preheat the grill and season the fish fillets with salt, pepper, and olive oil. Grill for 3 to 4 minutes on each side, then set aside to rest.
2. Heat the remaining 1 tablespoon of olive oil over medium heat in a large skillet. Add the minced garlic and cook until fragrant, about 1 minute.
3. Pour in the tomato puree and stir. Add the sugar (if using), oregano, thyme, and chilli flakes. Simmer the sauce for 8 to 10 minutes, until slightly thickened. Toss the grilled fish with the sauce, simmer for 2-3 minutes, and serve hot, garnished.

### PER SERVING:
Calories: 250 kcal; Fats: 12 g; Protein: 25 g; Carbs: 8 g; Sugar: 4 g; Fiber: 2 g

# GRILLED SALMON WITH VEGETABLES

## INGREDIENTS:

- 8 oz (230 g) salmon fillets
- 1 cup (150 g) broccoli florets
- 1/2 cup (75 g) baby carrots
- 1/2 cup (75 g) green peas
- 1/2 cup (75 g) mini corn, cut into pieces
- 1 tablespoon (15 ml) olive oil
- 1 teaspoon (5 ml) lemon juice
- Salt and pepper, to taste
- 1/2 teaspoon (2 g) garlic powder
- Fresh dill or parsley, for garnish

## INSTRUCTIONS:

1. Preheat the grill to medium heat. Brush the salmon fillets with olive oil and season them with salt, pepper, and garlic powder.
2. Place the salmon fillets on the grill and cook for 4–5 minutes per side, or until the fish is cooked and flakes easily with a fork.
3. Steam the broccoli, carrots, green peas, and mini corn over boiling water for 5–7 minutes, until tender but still crisp.
4. Serve the grilled salmon hot, accompanied by the steamed vegetables.

### PER SERVING:

Calories: 220 kcal; Fats: 12 g; Protein: 20 g; Carbs: 8 g; Sugar: 3 g; Fiber: 3 g

2 Portion    Easy    5 min    15 min

2 Portion    Easy    15 min    10 min

# SEARED TUNA COATED

## INGREDIENTS:

- 2 tuna steaks (400 g)
- 2 tablespoons (30 ml) olive oil
- 1 teaspoon (5 g) garlic powder
- 1 teaspoon (5 g) paprika
- Salt and pepper, to taste
- Green onions, sliced (for garnish)
- Lemon slices (for garnish)

## INSTRUCTIONS:

1. Inspect the tuna steaks for bones and remove them with tweezers necessary. Season the tuna steaks evenly with garlic powder, paprika, salt, and pepper. Drizzle with olive oil, ensuring the steaks are evenly coated, and let them rest for 15 minutes to allow the flavors to absorb.
2. Preheat a grill or grill pan to medium-high heat. Place the tuna steaks on the grill and cook for 4–5 minutes per side for medium-rare, adjusting the cooking time as needed to achieve your preferred level of doneness.
3. Transfer the seared tuna steaks to a serving plate. Garnish with chopped green onions and lemon slices for a bright and fresh finish. Serve hot and enjoy!

### PER SERVING:

Calories: 200 kcal; Fats: 12 g; Protein: 25 g; Carbs: 1 g; Sugar: 0 g; Fiber: 0 g

# CHAPTER 6   MEAT & POULTRY

# GRILLED PORK STEAK

**4 Portion**  **Easy**  **10 min**  **20 min**

## INGREDIENTS:

- 4 steaks (450 g) of pork tenderloin
- 2 tablespoons (30 ml) olive oil or butter
- Salt and pepper, to taste
- 1 tablespoon (15 g) fresh thyme (or 1 teaspoon dried thyme)
- 1/2 cup (120 ml) heavy cream

- 2 tablespoons (30 g) Dijon mustard
- 1 tablespoon (15 g) whole-grain mustard
- 1 teaspoon (5 ml) apple cider vinegar
- 1 tablespoon (15 ml) butter
- Salt and pepper, to taste

## INSTRUCTIONS:

1. Preheat your grill to medium-high heat.
2. Season the pork steaks with salt, pepper, and thyme. Brush both sides of the steaks with olive oil or melted butter.
3. Place the steaks on the grill and cook for 3–4 minutes per side, or until grill marks appear and the internal temperature reaches 145°F (65°C). Once cooked, transfer the steaks to a plate and let them rest for 5 minutes.
4. While the steaks are grilling, prepare the mustard sauce. Melt butter in a small saucepan over medium heat. Add heavy cream, Dijon mustard, whole-grain mustard, and apple cider vinegar. Stir well and let the sauce simmer for 2–3 minutes, until slightly thickened. Season with salt and pepper to taste. Serve the grilled pork steaks hot, drizzled with the mustard sauce.

**PER SERVING:**
Calories: 310 kcal; Fats: 22 g; Protein: 28 g; Carbs: 3 g; Sugar: 1 g; Fiber: 0 g

# GRILLED TURKEY WITH SALAD

## INGREDIENTS:

- 4 turkey fillets (400 g)
- 2 tablespoons (30 ml) olive oil
- 1 tablespoon (15 ml) lemon juice
- 1 teaspoon (5 g) paprika
- 1/2 teaspoon (2 g) garlic powder
- Salt and pepper, to taste
- 2 cups (100 g) spinach leaves
- 2 cups (100 g) arugula
- 1 cup (150 g) cherry tomatoes
- 1 avocado (150 g), sliced
- 2 tablespoons (30 ml) balsamic vinegar
- 2 tablespoons (30 ml) olive oil
- Salt and pepper, to taste

## INSTRUCTIONS:

1. Preheat the grill and season the turkey breasts with olive oil, lemon juice, and spices.
2. Grill the turkey on each side for 4-5 minutes, or until cooked through, then let it rest.
3. While the turkey is grilling, prepare the salad. Combine spinach, arugula, cherry tomatoes, and avocado slices in a bowl, tossed with balsamic vinaigrette. Serve the turkey breasts hot with the salad.

## PER SERVING:

Calories: 320 kcal; Fats: 20 g; Protein: 27 g; Carbs: 6 g; Sugar: 2 g; Fiber: 3 g

| 4 Portion | Easy | 15 min | 10 min |
| --- | --- | --- | --- |
| 2 Portion | Easy | 10 min | 10 min |

# MEATBALLS WITH TOMATOES

## INGREDIENTS:

- 1 lb (450 g) ground chicken
- 1/4 cup (60 g) almond flour
- 1 large egg (60 g)
- 2 cloves (10 g) garlic, minced
- 1 teaspoon (15 g) dried oregano
- 1 teaspoon (5 g) onion powder
- Salt and pepper, to taste
- 1 cup (140 g) tomatoes, finely chopped
- 2 tablespoons (30 g) fresh herbs
- 2 tablespoons (30 ml) olive oil

## INSTRUCTIONS:

1. Combine ground chicken, almond flour, egg, garlic, oregano, onion powder, salt, pepper, chopped tomatoes, and herbs in a large bowl. Mix until the ingredients are evenly combined.
2. Shape the mixture into small meatballs or patties.
3. Heat olive oil in a skillet over medium heat. Add the meatballs and cook for 5–7 minutes on each side, until they are golden brown and fully cooked.
4. Serve the meatballs hot, garnished with additional fresh herbs if desired.

## PER SERVING:

Calories: 250 kcal; Fats: 16 g; Protein: 23 g; Carbs: 5 g; Sugar: 2 g; Fiber: 1 g

# CHICKEN FILLET WITH ZUCCHINI GRILL

## INGREDIENTS:

- 10 ounces (280 g) chicken breast fillet, skinless and boneless
- 2 1/2 cups (300 g) zucchini, sliced into thin rounds
- 2 teaspoons (10 ml) lemon juice
- 1 teaspoon (5 ml) olive oil (for grilling)
- Salt and pepper, to taste
- Fresh basil leaves, for garnis

## INSTRUCTIONS:

1. Preheat a pan or outdoor grill and season the chicken fillet a zucchini slices with olive oil, salt, and pepper.
2. Place the chicken fillet on the hot grill and cook for 6–7 minutes p side, or until the internal temperature reaches 165°F (74°C Transfer to a plate and cover with foil to retain warmth. Grill t zucchini slices on each side for 2–3 minutes, or until they are tend and develop light grill marks.
3. Serve with a drizzle of lemon juice and garnish with basil.

PER SERVING:
Calories: 230 kcal; Fats: 8 g; Protein: 29 g; Carbs: 6 g; Sugar: 4 g; Fiber: 2 g

**2 Portion    Easy    10 min    15 min**

**2 Portion    Easy    15 min    20 min**

# GRILLED BEEF CHOPS

## INGREDIENTS:

- 4 beef chops (600 g)
- 2 tablespoons (30 ml) olive oil
- 1 teaspoon (5 g) garlic powder
- 1 teaspoon (5 g) smoked paprika
- 1 teaspoon (2 g) dried thyme
- Salt and pepper, to taste
- Fresh parsley, for garnish
- 3 cups (150 g) spinach leaves
- 1 1/2 cups (225 g) cherry tomatoes, halved
- 1 tablespoon (15 ml) lemon jui
- 2 tablespoons (30 ml) olive oil

## INSTRUCTIONS:

1. Preheat the grill. Brush beef chops evenly with olive oil. Seaso both sides with garlic powder, onion powder, smoked paprik dried thyme, salt, and pepper.
2. Place the beef chops on a hot grill and cook until the interna temperature reaches 135°F (57°C) for medium or 145°F (63°C) fo medium-well, 6 to 8 minutes per side. Remove chops from the gri and rest for 5 minutes. While the beef chops are resting, toss th baby spinach and halved cherry tomatoes in a bowl.
3. Whisk together the lemon juice, olive oil, salt, and pepper, an drizzle over the salad, tossing to coat. Serve beef chops hot.

PER SERVING:
Calories: 360 kcal; Fats: 22 g; Protein: 34 g; Carbs: 8 g; Sugar: 4 g; Fiber: 2 g

# OVEN BAKED RABBIT LEGS

**2 Portion   Medium   20 min   45 min**

## INGREDIENTS:

- 4 rabbit legs (800 g)
- 2 tablespoons (30 ml) olive oil
- 2 cloves (10 g) garlic, minced
- 1 teaspoon (5 g) dried thyme
- 1 teaspoon (5 g) smoked paprika

- 1 teaspoon (5 g) onion powder
- 1/2 cup (120 ml) dry white wine (optional)
- Salt and pepper, to taste
- 1 cup (150 g) green peas, for garnish

## INSTRUCTIONS:

1. Preheat the oven to 375°F (190°C).
2. In a bowl, combine olive oil, minced garlic, thyme, smoked paprika, onion powder, salt, and pepper. Mix well to create an aromatic marinade. Brush the mixture evenly over both sides of the rabbit legs, ensuring they are fully coated for maximum flavor. Let the rabbit legs sit at room temperature for 10 minutes to allow the marinade to infuse.
3. Place the seasoned rabbit legs into a baking dish in a single layer. If using white wine, pour it around the legs of the dish to keep them moist and enhance the flavor. Cover the dish tightly with aluminum foil and bake for 30 minutes to trap the juices. Rotate the baking dish halfway through the cooking time to ensure even heating.
4. After 30 minutes, remove the foil and return the dish to the oven. Continue baking for an additional 10–15 minutes, or until the rabbit legs are golden brown and have reached an internal temperature of 160°F (71 °C).
5. Serve the rabbit legs hot on a plate, garnished with vibrant green peas for a fresh finishing touch.

**PER SERVING:**
Calories: 320 kcal; Fats: 18 g; Protein: 35 g; Carbs: 4 g; Sugar: 2 g; Fiber: 1 g

# BAKED CHICKEN ROLL

## INGREDIENTS:

- 1 large (300 g) chicken breast
- 1 small (70 g) onion, finely chopped
- 2 cloves (10 g) garlic, minced
- 2 tablespoons (30 ml) extra virgin olive oil
- Salt and pepper, to taste
- 1 teaspoon (2 g) dried thyme

## INSTRUCTIONS:

1. Preheat the oven to 375°F (190 °C). Pounded the chicken breasts with a mallet until they were uniformly thick.
2. In a bowl, combine the finely chopped onion, crushed garlic, olive oil, dried thyme, salt, and pepper. Mix thoroughly.
3. Spread the mixture evenly over the chicken breasts. Roll up tightly and secure with toothpicks.
4. Heat a frying pan over medium heat. Brown the chicken breasts on all sides, about 3–4 minutes per side. Transfer the breasts to a baking dish and bake in the oven for 25 minutes.
5. Let the breasts rest for 5 minutes before slicing. Serve hot.

### PER SERVING:
Calories: 250 kcal; Fats: 13 g; Protein: 25 g; Carbs: 5 g; Sugar: 3 g; Fiber: 1 g

**2 Portion    Easy    5 min    15 min**

**2 Portion    Easy    15 min    25 min**

# FETA STUFFED BREASTS

## INGREDIENTS:

- 2 fillets (30 g) of chicken
- 1/2 cup (70 g) cottage cheese
- 1/2 cup (70 g) ricotta cheese
- 1/4 cup (10 g) fresh parsley
- 1 tablespoon (2 g) fresh basil, chopped
- 1 teaspoon (5 g) garlic powder
- 1 teaspoon (5 g) onion powder
- Salt and pepper, to taste
- 2 tablespoons (30 ml) olive oil
- 1/2 cup (70 g) grated Parmesan cheese (optional, for topping)

## INSTRUCTIONS:

1. Preheat oven to 375°F (190°C).
2. Combine cottage cheese, ricotta cheese, parsley, basil, garlic powder, onion powder, salt, and pepper in a bowl. Mix thoroughly.
3. Cut pockets in the chicken breasts and fill them with the prepared cheese mixture. Heat olive oil in a skillet. Brown the stuffed chicken breasts for 3-4 minutes on each side, turning them occasionally.
4. Transfer the browned chicken breasts to a baking dish. Sprinkle with Parmesan cheese, and bake in the oven for 15-20 minutes until cooked. Serve hot.

### PER SERVING:
Calories: 370 kcal; Fats: 22 g; Protein: 38 g; Carbs: 5 g; Sugar: 2 g; Fiber: 0.5 g

# TURKEY STUFFED WITH SPINACH

**2 Portion**   **Easy**   **20 min**   **30 min**

## INGREDIENTS:

- 2 fillets (300 g) of turkey
- 2 tablespoons (30 ml) olive oil
- 1 tablespoon (15 ml) lemon juice
- Salt and pepper, to taste
- 1 cup (100 g) fresh spinach

- 1/4 cup (60 g) cream cheese
- 1/4 cup (30 g) shredded hard cheese, such as cheddar or Parmesan
- 2 cloves (10 g) garlic, minced
- 1 cup (50 g) mixed salad greens

## INSTRUCTIONS:

1. Preheat the oven to 375°F (190°C).
2. Pat the turkey fillets dry with paper towels. Gently pound them with a meat mallet until thin and even. Season with salt, pepper, and lemon juice.
3. Heat 1 tablespoon (15 ml) olive oil in a skillet over medium heat. Add the minced garlic and fresh spinach. Sauté for 2–3 minutes, stirring frequently, until the spinach wilts. Remove from heat. Combine the sautéed spinach with cream cheese and shredded hard cheese in a bowl. Mix thoroughly and season the filling with salt and pepper, to taste.
4. Spread the filling evenly over each turkey fillet. Roll each fillet tightly into a roulade and secure with toothpicks or kitchen twine.
5. Heat the remaining tablespoon (15 ml) of olive oil in the same skillet over medium heat. Brown the roulades on all sides for about 3–4 minutes.
6. Transfer the browned roulades to a baking dish. Bake in the oven for 10–12 minutes, or until the turkey is fully cooked. Let the roulades rest for 5 minutes before removing the toothpicks or twine. Slice the roulades into medallions and serve with mixed salad greens.

### PER SERVING:
Calories: 320 kcal; Fats: 18 g; Protein: 35 g; Carbs: 3 g; Sugar: 1 g; Fiber: 1 g

# DUCK BREAST WITH ORANGE SAUCE

## INGREDIENTS:

- 2 duck breast fillets with skin (approximately 300 g)
- Salt and pepper, to taste
- 1/2 cup (120 ml) orange juice
- 1 tablespoon (15 g) honey
- 1 tablespoon (15 ml) soy sauce
- 1 tablespoon (15 ml) balsamic vinegar
- Zest of 1 orange
- 1 tablespoon (15 g) butter
- Salt and pepper, to taste
- 1 cup (50 g) mixed salad greens

## INSTRUCTIONS:

1. Preheat the oven to 190°C.
2. Prepare the duck breasts by scoring the skin and seasoning with s and pepper. Place the duck breasts skin-side down in the pan a cook for 6–7 minutes. Turn the fillets over and cook for a further 3 minutes. Then bake for 8–10 minutes for medium-rare.
3. Meanwhile, make the orange sauce by simmering the orange jui honey, soy sauce, balsamic vinegar, and zest until thickened.
4. Serve the duck breasts drizzled with the sauce and mixed spices.

### PER SERVING:
Calories: 400 kcal; Fats: 25 g; Protein: 35 g; Carbs: 10 g; Sugar: 8 g; Fiber: (

**2 Portion**   **Easy**   **10 min**   **25 min**

**2 Portion**   **Easy**   **15 min**   **25 min**

# TURKEY WITH VEGETABLES

## INGREDIENTS:

- 1 lb (450 g) turkey fillets
- 1 cup (120 g) green asparagus beans
- 1 tablespoon (15 g) honey
- 1 teaspoon (5 g) garlic powder
- 1 medium (80 g) onion, sliced
- 2 tablespoons (30 ml) olive oil
- 2 tablespoons (30 ml) soy sauce
- 1 medium yellow bell pepper
- 1 medium red bell pepper, slice
- 1 teaspoon (5 g) smoked paprik
- Salt and pepper, to taste

## INSTRUCTIONS:

1. Heat 1 tablespoon olive oil. Add turkey strips and cook for 5- minutes, until cooked through. Remove turkey and set aside.
2. To the same pan, add the remaining 1 tablespoon olive oil. Saut the sliced onion, then add the red and yellow bell peppers alon with the green beans. Cook for another 5-6 minutes, stirrin occasionally, until the vegetables are soft but still slightly crisp.
3. In a bowl, combine the soy sauce, honey, garlic powder, smoke paprika, salt, and pepper. Pour sauce into pan and stir. Add cooke turkey back to skillet. Cook for another 2-3 minutes. Adjus seasonings. Serve hot.

### PER SERVING:
Calories: 290 kcal; Fats: 10 g; Protein: 30 g; Carbs: 12 g; Sugar: 6 g; Fiber: 3

SIDE DISHES & VEGGIES

# BEANS WITH TOMATOES AND HERBS

**4 Portion**  **Easy**  **15 min**  **5 min**

## INGREDIENTS:

- 240 g (1 cup) canned white beans, rinsed and drained
- 200 g (1 cup) cherry tomatoes, halved
- 100 g (1 small) red onion, thinly sliced
- 15 ml (1 tablespoon) olive oil
- 15 ml (1 tablespoon) lemon juice

- 1 garlic clove, minced
- 2 g (1/2 teaspoon) dried oregano
- Salt and pepper to taste
- 15 g (1/4 cup) fresh parsley, chopped
- 10 g (2 tablespoons) fresh basil, chopped (optional)

## INSTRUCTIONS:

1. Place the white beans, cherry tomatoes, and red onion in a large mixing bowl. Drain the beans well so the salad doesn't become watery.
2. Whisk together the olive oil, lemon juice, minced garlic, oregano, salt, and pepper in a small bowl until well combined and smooth. Let the dressing sit for a minute to allow the flavors to blend.
3. Pour the dressing over the salad and gently toss everything together. Stir carefully to keep the beans whole and the tomatoes from breaking apart.
4. Add the chopped parsley and basil, then mix until the herbs are evenly distributed. For best results, chill the salad for 15–20 minutes before serving.
5. Serve cold or at room temperature.
6. This fresh, colorful salad makes a great side dish or light lunch.

**PER SERVING:**
Calories: 160 kcal; Fats: 5g; Protein: 7g; Carbs: 20g; Sugar: 4g; Fiber: 5g

# BULGUR PILAF WITH CHICKEN

## INGREDIENTS:

- 150 g (5.3 ounces) bulgur
- 300 g (10.5 ounces) skinless chicken breast, diced
- 1 medium onion, finely chopped
- 1 medium carrot, grated
- 1 bell pepper, diced
- 2 tablespoons olive oil
- 1 teaspoon ground turmeric
- ½ teaspoon ground cumin
- 1 teaspoon paprika
- 500 ml (2 cups) low-sodium chicken broth or water
- Salt and pepper, to taste
- Fresh parsley (for garnish)

## INSTRUCTIONS:

1. Heat 1 tablespoon olive oil over medium heat in a large non-stick skillet. Cook the chicken until it is browned (5–7 minutes), then set it aside. Add remaining oil, onion, carrots, and bell pepper; fry for 5 minutes, then add turmeric, cumin, paprika and bulgur.
2. Toast for 1–2 minutes. Return the chicken, add broth, season, bring to a boil, cover, and simmer on low for 15–18 minutes.
3. Rest for 5 minutes off the heat, and garnish with parsley.

### PER SERVING:

Calories: 330 kcal; Fats: 9g; Protein: 30g; Carbs: 33g; Sugar: 4g; Fiber: 5g

# BEANS IN TOMATO SAUCE

## INGREDIENTS:

- 2 cups (330 g) cooked white beans (cannellini or navy)
- 1 medium onion, finely chopped
- 2 garlic cloves, minced
- 400 g (14 ounces) canned crushed tomatoes (no added salt)
- 1 tablespoon olive oil
- 1 teaspoon smoked paprika
- ½ teaspoon dried oregano
- ½ teaspoon ground black pepper
- Salt, to taste
- Fresh parsley (for garnish)

## INSTRUCTIONS:

1. Heat olive oil in a non-stick skillet over medium heat. Add onion and garlic, and sauté for 4–5 minutes until soft.
2. Stir in crushed tomatoes, paprika, oregano, pepper, and salt. Simmer for 10 minutes, stirring occasionally, until the sauce has thickened.
3. Add cooked beans and mix well to coat them in the sauce.
4. Lower the heat and simmer for an additional 5–7 minutes, allowing the flavors to combine and the beans to heat through. Remove from heat and garnish with chopped basil or parsley before serving.

### PER SERVING:

Calories: 210 kcal; Fats: 5g; Protein: 10g; Carbs: 30g; Sugar: 6g; Fiber: 8g

| 4 Portion | Mediu m | 10 min | 25 min |
| --- | --- | --- | --- |
| 4 Portion | Easy | 10 min | 20 min |

# HUMMUS WITH VEGETABLE STICKS

### INGREDIENTS:

- 1½ cups (250 g) cooked chickpeas
- 2 tablespoons tahini
- 2 tablespoons lemon juice
- 1 garlic clove, minced
- 2 tablespoons cold water
- 1 tablespoon olive oil
- ½ teaspoon ground cumin
- Salt, to taste
- Paprika (for garnish)
- Raw vegetable sticks (carrot, cucumber, celery, bell pepper)

### INSTRUCTIONS:

1. Combine chickpeas, tahini, lemon juice, garlic, cumin, and salt in food processor. Blend until smooth.
2. Gradually add cold water while blending until the hummus reaches a creamy consistency.
3. Transfer the hummus to a serving bowl and smooth the top .
4. Drizzle with olive oil and sprinkle with paprika before serving.
5. Serve with fresh vegetable sticks, such as carrots, cucumber, celery, and bell peppers.

### PER SERVING:
Calories: 180 kcal; Fats: 9g; Protein: 6g; Carbs: 18g; Sugar: 3g; Fiber: 5g

**4 Portion   Easy   10 min   0 min**

**4 Portion   Easy   5 min   10 min**

# QUINOA WITH PISTACHIOS

### INGREDIENTS:

- 1 cup (170 g) quinoa
- 2 cups (480 ml) water or low-sodium vegetable broth
- ½ cup (60 g) unsalted pistachios, roughly chopped
- 2 tablespoons olive oil
- 1 small red onion, finely chopped
- 1 garlic clove, minced
- Zest and juice of ½ lemon
- Salt and pepper, to taste
- Fresh mint or parsley (for garnish)

### INSTRUCTIONS:

1. Rinse the quinoa thoroughly under cold water.
2. In a saucepan, bring water or broth to a boil, then add the quinoa. Reduce the heat, cover, and simmer for 15 minutes, or until the quinoa is tender and the liquid is absorbed.
3. Fluff the cooked quinoa with a fork, then stir in the onion mixture, lemon zest, lemon juice, salt, and pepper.
4. Fold in chopped pistachios and garnish with fresh mint or parsley before serving.

### PER SERVING:
Calories: 290 kcal; Fats: 14g; Protein: 8g; Carbs: 30g; Sugar: 2g; Fiber: 4g

# CURRY WITH CHICKPEAS

**2 Portion**  **Medium**  **15 min**  **20 min**

## INGREDIENTS:

- 240 g (1 cup) canned chickpeas
- 400 ml (1 can / 14 oz) coconut milk
- 100 g (1 small) onion, diced
- 2 garlic cloves, minced
- 15 g (1 tablespoon) grated ginger
- 60 g (1 small) sliced carrot
- 100 g (1 small) diced bell pepper
- 14 g (2 tablespoons) curry powder
- 15 g (1 tablespoon) tomato paste
- 15 ml (1 tablespoon) olive oil
- 2 g (1/2 teaspoon) cumin powder
- Salt and pepper to taste
- Fresh cilantro, chopped (optional for garnish)

## INSTRUCTIONS:

1. Heat olive oil in a large skillet over medium heat.
2. Add diced onion and cook for 3–4 minutes until soft.
3. Add minced garlic and grated ginger, and cook for an additional 1–2 minutes, until fragrant.
4. Stir in curry powder, cumin powder, and tomato paste. Cook for 1 minute, stirring constantly.
5. Add sliced carrot and diced bell pepper to the skillet. Cook for 5–7 minutes, or until the vegetables are tender.
6. Add chickpeas and coconut milk to the skillet. Bring to a simmer and cook for 10–15 minutes, or until the sauce has thickened.
7. Stir occasionally to prevent sticking and ensure even cooking.
8. Season with salt and pepper to taste. Garnish with chopped cilantro, if desired, and serve immediately.

**PER SERVING:**
Calories: 420 kcal; Fats: 22g; Protein: 12g; Carbs: 45g; Sugar: 8g; Fiber: 12g

# WILD RICE WITH GREEN BEANS, CARROTS

**4 Portion**  **Medium**  **10 min**  **40 min.**

## INGREDIENTS:

- 185 g (1 cup) wild rice
- 480 ml (2 cups) vegetable broth
- 150 g (1 cup) green beans, trimmed and cut into 2.5 cm (1-inch) pieces
- 130 g (1 cup) carrots, sliced
- 15 ml (1 tablespoon) olive oil
- 2 g (1/2 teaspoon) garlic powder
- Salt and pepper to taste
- Fresh parsley, chopped (optional for garnish)

## INSTRUCTIONS:

1. Rinse the wild rice under cold water, then place it in a saucepan with the vegetable broth. Bring to a boil over medium heat.
2. Reduce the heat to low, cover, and simmer for 35–40 minutes until the rice is tender and the liquid is absorbed. Remove from heat and let stand, covered, for 5 minutes.
3. While the rice is cooking, heat the olive oil in a skillet over medium heat. Add the sliced carrots and cook for about 5 minutes, stirring occasionally.
4. Add the green beans and garlic powder, then cook for an additional 5–7 minutes, until the vegetables are tender but still crisp. Season with salt and pepper.
5. Fluff the cooked rice with a fork and combine it with the sautéed vegetables in a large bowl. Stir well to mix everything evenly.
6. Garnish with chopped parsley before serving. This dish can be served warm or at room temperature.

**PER SERVING:**
Calories: 220 kcal; Fats: 6g; Protein: 6g; Carbs: 36g; Sugar: 4g; Fiber: 5g

# CRISPY BRUSSELS SPROUTS

**INGREDIENTS:**

- 500 g (1.1 lb) Brussels sprouts, trimmed and halved
- 2 tablespoons olive oil
- 1 teaspoon garlic powder
- ½ teaspoon smoked paprika
- Salt and pepper, to taste
- 1 tablespoon lemon juice (optional)
- Fresh parsley (for garnish)

**INSTRUCTIONS:**

1. Rinse Brussels sprouts and pat them dry with a clean towel.
2. Preheat the oven to 200°C (400°F) and line a baking sheet with parchment paper.
3. Toss Brussels sprouts with olive oil, garlic powder, paprika, salt, and pepper in a large bowl.
4. Spread evenly on the baking sheet, cut-side down, and roast for 20–25 minutes, until golden brown and crispy on the edges.
5. Remove from oven, drizzle with lemon juice if desired, and garnish with chopped parsley before serving.

**PER SERVING:**

Calories: 130 kcal; Fats: 7g; Protein: 4g; Carbs: 13g; Sugar: 3g; Fiber: 5g

| 4 Portion | Easy | 10 min | 25 min |
|-----------|------|--------|--------|
| 4 Portion | Easy | 5 min | 45 min |

# DELICIOUS BAKED SWEET POTATOES

**INGREDIENTS:**

- 4 medium sweet potatoes
- 1 tablespoon olive oil
- ½ teaspoon ground cinnamon (optional)
- Salt and pepper, to taste
- Fresh limon ,1 clice, (for garnish)
- Fresh herbs (thyme or parsley, for garnish)

**INSTRUCTIONS:**

1. Preheat the oven to 200°C (400°F) and line a baking sheet with parchment paper.
2. Wash sweet potatoes thoroughly and pat them dry.
3. Pierce each sweet potato several times with a fork.
4. Rub the skins with olive oil, season with salt, pepper, and cinnamon if using.
5. Place the cookies on the baking sheet and bake for 40–45 minutes, or until they are soft inside and crispy outside.
6. Remove from oven, let cool slightly, and garnish with fresh herbs before serving.

**PER SERVING:**

Calories: 180 kcal; Fats: 4g; Protein: 3g; Carbs: 35g; Sugar: 9g; Fiber: 5g

# CAULIFLOWER RICE WITH HERBS

## INGREDIENTS:

- medium head of cauliflower, cut into florets
- 1 tablespoon olive oil
- 1 garlic clove, minced
- Salt and pepper, to taste
- ¼ cup chopped fresh parsley
- 2 tablespoons chopped fresh dill
- 1 tablespoon lemon juice (optional)

## INSTRUCTIONS:

1. Pulse the cauliflower florets in a food processor until the textu[re] resembles that of rice.
2. Heat olive oil in a non-stick skillet over medium heat. Add garl[ic] and sauté for 1 minute.
3. Add cauliflower rice, season with salt and pepper, and cook for 5– minutes, stirring occasionally.
4. Stir in parsley, dill, and lemon juice if using.
5. Cook for 1–2 minutes, remove from heat, and serve warm.

### PER SERVING:
Calories: 70 kcal; Fats: 4g; Protein: 2g; Carbs: 6g; Sugar: 2g; Fiber: 3g

4 Portion | Easy | 10 min | 10 min

4 Portion | Easy | 10 min | 12 min

# ASPARAGUS WITH MUSHROOMS

## INGREDIENTS:

- 1 bunch (about 400 g) fresh asparagus, trimmed
- 200 g (7 ounces) cremini or button mushrooms, sliced
- 1 tablespoon olive oil
- 1 garlic clove, minced
- Salt and pepper, to taste
- 1 tablespoon lemon juice
- Fresh thyme or parsley (for garnish)

## INSTRUCTIONS:

1. Bring a pot of water to a boil. Blanch the asparagus for 2 minute[s] then transfer it to ice water to stop the cooking process. Drain a[nd] set aside.
2. In a large skillet, heat olive oil over medium heat. Add garlic a[nd] sauté for 30 seconds.
3. Add the mushrooms, season with salt and pepper, and cook for 6– minutes, until they are soft and golden.
4. Add the asparagus to the skillet and toss with the mushrooms for 2 3 minutes, until heated through. Drizzle with lemon juice a[nd] garnish with thyme or parsley before serving.

### PER SERVING:
Calories: 90 kcal; Fats: 5g; Protein: 4g; Carbs: 8g; Sugar: 3g; Fiber: 3g

**SNACKS & DRINKS**

# MINI CANAPES WITH SMOKED SALMON, SOFT CHEESE

**12 Portion**   **Easy**   **15 min**   **2 min**

## INGREDIENTS:

- 200 g (7 oz) smoked salmon, thinly sliced
- 150 g (5 oz) soft cream cheese, softened
- 12 slices of Keto Bread  (see p. 70)
- 1 lemon (for juice and zest)
- 15 g pea sprouts (for garnish)

- 15 g (1/4 cup) fresh dill, finely chopped
- 3 radish, julienned (for garnish)
- 15 g cucumber, julienned (for garnish)
- Freshly ground black pepper, to taste

## INSTRUCTIONS:

1. Preheat the oven to 180°C (350°F) and lightly toast the keto bread slices until crisp; once toasted, cut each slice into canapé-sized pieces if desired.
2. Next, prepare the filling. Sprinkle the smoked salmon slices with lemon juice. Pick fresh pea sprouts, then slice the radishes and cucumber into thin, tender strips. Layer the salmon slices and evenly distribute the pea sprouts, radishes, and cucumber over each slice. Once layered, carefully roll up the salmon slices, ensuring the crispy vegetables are sealed tightly and ready to add extra crunch to your dish.
3. Pour the cream cheese into a piping bag fitted with your favourite tip, or use a small spoon if you don't have a piping bag. Generously pipe a neat swirl of softened cream cheese onto each toasted slice of keto bread, creating a creamy base for the next layer. Place a rolled-up slice of smoked salmon on top of the cheese.

**PER SERVING:**

Calories: 120 kcal; Fats: 5g; Protein: 8g; Carbs: 10g; Sugar: 1g; Fiber: 1g

# SOUFFLÉ WITH RASPBERRIES

## INGREDIENTS:

- 300 g (10.5 oz) low-fat cottage cheese
- 2 egg whites
- 1 cup (240 ml) fat-free milk
- 1 teaspoon (5 ml) vanilla extract
- Sweetener to taste
- A pinch of salt
- Fresh raspberries (to garnish or gently fold in, if preferred)

## INSTRUCTIONS:

1. Preheat oven to 350°F (175°C) and prepare two small soufflé ramekins or cups by lightly greasing them.
2. Whisk together the cottage cheese, skim milk, vanilla extract, and sweetener until smooth.
3. In a separate bowl, beat the egg whites with a pinch of salt until stiff peaks form. Gently fold the beaten egg whites into the cheese mixture. Divide the mixture between the two cups and bake for 15 to 20 minutes, until the soufflé is golden on top.
4. Let cool slightly, then garnish with fresh raspberries.

## PER SERVING:

Calories: 280 kcal; Fats: 12g; Protein: 10g; Carbs: 32g; Sugar: 6g; Fiber: 8g

| 2 Portion | Easy | 10 min | 20 min |
|-----------|------|--------|--------|
| 2 Portion | Easy | 5 min | 0 min |

# CARROT AND ORANGE SMOOTHIE

## INGREDIENTS:

- 150 g total, (5.3 oz) medium carrots
- 1 large orange
- 1 cup (240 ml) water
- 1 teaspoon (7 g) honey or stevia
- Optional: 1/2 teaspoon grated fresh ginger

## INSTRUCTIONS:

1. Wash the carrots and orange thoroughly.
2. Peel the carrots and orange, then cut the carrots into small pieces and separate the orange into segments (removing any seeds).
3. Place the carrot pieces, orange segments, water, and, if using, grated ginger in a blender.
4. Blend on high speed until smooth and well combined.
5. Taste and, if needed, add your preferred sweetener; adjust the consistency with additional water or ice if desired.
6. Pour into glasses and serve immediately.

## PER SERVING:

Calories: 89 kcal; Fats: 0.3g; Protein: 1.6g; Carbs: 22g; Sugar: 15g; Fiber: 4.5g

# GREEN SMOOTHIE

## INGREDIENTS:

- ½ medium avocado
- 2 cups (60 g) fresh spinach leaves
- 1 medium apple, cored
- 1 tablespoon (15 g) chia seeds
- 1 cup (240 ml) water
- Juice of ½ lemon

## INSTRUCTIONS:

1. Thoroughly wash all produce.
2. Core the apple and cut it into chunks. Cut the avocado in hal remove the pit, and scoop out the flesh.
3. Place the avocado, apple chunks, spinach leaves, chia seeds, wate and (if using) lemon juice into a blender.
4. Blend on high speed until smooth; if desired, adjust the consistenc with extra water or a few ice cubes.
5. Pour into glasses and serve immediately.

### PER SERVING:
Calories: 170 kcal; Fats: 10g; Protein: 3g; Carbs: 21g; Sugars: 10g; Fiber: 9g

2 Portion    Easy    5 min    0 min

2 Portion    Easy    10 min    25 min

# OATMEAL ENERGY BARS

## INGREDIENTS:

- 90 g (1 cup) whole grain oats
- 75 g (1/2 cup) chopped dried figs
- 35 g (1/4 cup) chopped almonds
- 24 g (2 tablespoons) chia seeds
- 20 g (2 tablespoons) sunflower seeds
- 64 g (1/4 cup) almond butter
- 80 g (1/4 cup) honey
- 5 ml (1 teaspoon) vanilla extract
- 1.25 ml (1/4 teaspoon) sal
- 40 g (1/4 cup) dried cranberries

## INSTRUCTIONS:

1. Preheat the oven to 350°F (180°C) and line an 8x8-inch (20x20 cm pan with parchment paper.
2. In a large bowl, combine whole grain oats, chopped figs, choppe almonds, cranberries, chia seeds, and sunflower seeds.
3. In a small saucepan or microwave-safe bowl, gently melt the hone (or maple syrup) with the almond butter until smooth; then stir i the vanilla extract and salt. Pour the wet mixture over the dr ingredients and stir until evenly combined. Press the mixture firml into the prepared pan. Bake for 25 minutes, until the top is golden.
4. Let cool completely before removing and cutting into bars.

### PER SERVING:
Calories: 170 kcal; Fats: 6g; Protein: 3g; Carbs: 28g; Sugars: 12g; Fiber:4g

# COTTAGE CHEESE CHEESECAKES

## INGREDIENTS:

- 1 large egg
- 8 g (2 teaspoons) stevia
- 300 g (1 1/3 cups) cottage cheese
- 9 g (3 teaspoons) almond flour
- A pinch of salt
- 5 ml (1 teaspoon) vegetable oil
- 10 g (1 tablespoon) fresh raspberries (for finishing)
- 10 g (1 tablespoon) fresh blueberries (for finishing)
- Mint leaves (for finishing)

## INSTRUCTIONS:

1. Mix the cottage cheese, egg, stevia, almond flour, and a pinch of salt until smooth.
2. Form the mixture into balls about 5 cm in diameter and press them down to form smooth cheesecakes. Roll each cheesecake in almond flour to keep its shape. Heat the oil in a frying pan and fry the cheesecakes for 2-3 minutes on each side until golden brown.
3. Garnish the finished cheesecakes with fresh raspberries, blueberries, and mint leaves. Serve warm.

### PER SERVING:
Calories: 138 kcal; Fats: 6.5g; Protein: 10g; Carbs: 7.5g; Sugars: 2.5g; Fiber: 1g

**4 Portion**　**Easy**　**10 min**　**10 min**

**2 Portion**　**Easy**　**10 min**　**10 min**

# AVOCADO AND BANANA SMOOTHIE

## INGREDIENTS:

- 250 g (2 medium) ripe bananas
- 200 ml (3/4 cup + 2 tablespoons) plain unsweetened yogurt
- 150 ml (2/3 cup) water or ice
- 30 ml (2 tablespoons) lime juice
- 100 g (1/2 medium) avocado
- 1 vanilla bean (or 1/2 teaspoon vanilla extract)
- 10 g (1 tablespoon) honey or stevia to taste (optional)

## INSTRUCTIONS:

1. Slice the avocado in half, remove the pit, and scoop out the flesh.
2. Peel the bananas and cut them into chunks.
3. Scrape the seeds from the vanilla bean, or use vanilla extract instead.
4. Combine the avocado, banana chunks, yogurt, lime juice, vanilla, and water (or ice) in a blender. Add optional honey or stevia for additional sweetness, if desired.
5. Blend on high speed until smooth and creamy. Adjust the consistency by adding more water if necessary.
6. Pour into glasses and serve immediately.

### PER SERVING:
Calories: 198 kcal; Fats: 7g; Protein: 4g; Carbs: 30g; Sugars: 21g; Fiber: 4g

# BAKED PEAR WITH CHEESE

## INGREDIENTS:

- 4 medium ripe pears
- 1/2 cup (120 g) gorgonzola cheese
- 2 tablespoons (30 g) blue cheese
- 1/4 cup (60 ml) honey
- 1/4 cup (30 g) chopped walnuts
- Fresh thyme leaves (for garnish)

## INSTRUCTIONS:

1. Preheat the oven to 175°C (350°F), and line a baking dish with parchment paper. Cut the pears in half and remove the cores.
2. Stuff the pears with the cheese and honey mixture and bake for 20 minutes, until the pears are soft and the cheese has melted.
3. Leave to cool slightly, garnish with thyme leaves, and serve warm.

### PER SERVING:

Calories: 320 kcal; Fats: 20g; Protein: 8g; Carbs: 28g; Sugars: 24g; Fiber: 3g

| 4 Portion | Easy | 5 min | 20 min |
|---|---|---|---|
| 2 Portion | Easy | 2 min | 0 min |

# JUICY APPLES WITH ALMONDS

## INGREDIENTS:

- 2 medium apples (150–180 g)
- 2 (14 g) almonds (optional)

## INSTRUCTIONS:

1. Peel the apples and slice them. Serve with almonds if desired.

## EFFECT:

It actively helps reduce the level of "bad" cholesterol (LDL) in the blood, promotes healthy blood vessels, and reduces inflammation.

### PER SERVING:

Calories: 105 kcal; Fats: 2g; Protein: 1g; Carbs: 24g; Sugars: 18g; Fiber: 6.5g

| 2 Portion | Easy | 2 min | 0 min |
|---|---|---|---|
| 2 Portion | Easy | 2 min | 10 min |

# FRUIT SALAD WITH WALNUTS

## INGREDIENTS:

- 1 medium orange, segmented
- 2 medium kiwis, sliced
- 1 medium banana, sliced
- 2 tablespoons (30 g) walnuts
- 1/4 cup (60 g) pomegranate arils
- 1 teaspoon (10 g) chia seeds
- 1 teaspoon (10 g) honey (optional)
- 1 teaspoon (10 g) fresh lime juice

## INSTRUCTIONS:

1. Peel and segment the orange, slice the kiwis and banana, and gather the pomegranate arils. In a bowl, mix the fruits, then top with chopped walnuts and chia seeds.
2. Drizzle with honey or lime juice if desired, toss gently, and serve immediately.

### PER SERVING:

Calories: 180 kcal; Fats: 7g; Protein: 3g; Carbs: 30g; Sugars: 18g; Fiber: 6g

# STUFFED BAKED APPLES

**INGREDIENTS:**

- 4 large apples
- 240 g (1 cup) cottage cheese
- 40 g (1/4 cup) raisins
- 15 ml (1 tablespoon) honey
- 30 g (1/4 cup) chopped walnuts
- 15 ml (1 tablespoon) coconut oil

**INSTRUCTIONS:**

1. Preheat the oven to 180ºC (350ºF) and grease a baking dish with coconut oil. Core the apples, leaving the bottom intact to create a cavity for the filling.
2. Mix the cottage cheese, raisins, honey and chopped walnuts, then fill the apples. Bake for 30 minutes until done.

**PER SERVING:**

Calories: 258 kcal; Fats: 7g; Protein: 8g; Carbs: 48g; Sugars: 38g; Fiber: 5g

| 4 Portion | Easy | 0 min | 0 min |
|-----------|------|-------|-------|
| 2 Portion | Easy | 2 min | 10 min |

# JUICY PEAR WITH HONEY

**INGREDIENTS:**

- 2 medium pears (150–180 g)
- 2 (14 g) teaspoons honey (optional)

**INSTRUCTIONS:**

1. Peel the pear and cut it into portions. Serve with honey if desired.

**EFFECT:**

Improved digestion, reduced sugar and cholesterol levels, strengthened the immune system, and maintained cardiovascular health.

**PER SERVING:**

Calories: 85 kcal; Fats: 0g; Protein: 0.5g; Carbs: 22g; Sugars: 16g; Fiber: 6g

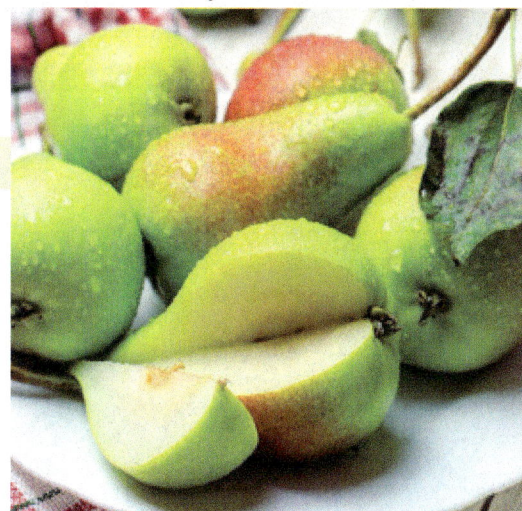

| 2 Portion | Easy | 2 min | 0 min |
|-----------|------|-------|-------|
| 2 Portion | Easy | 2 min | 10 min |

# SALAD WITH PLUMS AND APPLE

**INGREDIENTS:**

- 120 g (4 cups) mixed leafy greens
- 150 g (2 medium) plums
- 100 g (1 medium) apple
- 30 g (2 tablespoons) pecans
- 15 ml (1 tablespoon) olive oil
- 10 ml (2 teaspoons) balsamic vinegar
- 5 g (1 teaspoon) honey
- Salt and black pepper to taste

**INSTRUCTIONS:**

1. Thinly slice the plums and apples. Combine the leafy greens, sliced plums, apples, and chopped nuts in a bowl.
2. Mix the olive oil, balsamic vinegar, honey, salt, and pepper to make the dressing. Drizzle the dressing over the salad and toss to combine. Serve immediately.

**PER SERVING:**

Calories: 188 kcal; Fats: 10g; Protein: 2.5g; Carbs: 24g; Sugars: 19g; Fiber: 4g

# AROMATIC LINDEN TEA

## INGREDIENTS:

- 2 teaspoons (10 g) dried linden flowers
- 500 ml (2 cups) boiling water

## INSTRUCTIONS:

1. Add dried linden flowers to the teapot.
2. Pour boiling water over the linden flowers and steep them for 7 minutes. Strain the tea into cups and serve with honey or lemon.

### PER SERVING:
Calories: 22 kcal; Fats: 0g; Protein: 0g; Carbs: 6g; Sugars: 6g; Fiber: 0g

2 Portion | Easy | 5 min | 7 min

# ROSEHIP DRINK

2 Portion | Easy | 5 min | 15 min

## INGREDIENTS:

- 2 tablespoons (20 g) dried rosehips
- 2 cups (500 ml) boiling wate

## INSTRUCTIONS:

1. Add the dried rosehips to a teapot. Pour boiling water over the rosehips and allow them to steep for 10–15 minutes.
2. Strain the drink into cups and add honey or lemon if desired.
3. Serve warm or let it cool for a refreshing chilled version.

### PER SERVING:
Calories: 22 kcal; Fats: 0g; Protein: 0g; Carbs: 6g; Sugars: 6g; Fiber: 0g

2 Portion | Easy | 5 min | 5 min

# REFRESHING MINT TEA

## INGREDIENTS:

- 2 tablespoons (10 g) mint leaves
- 2 cups (500 ml) boiling wate

## INSTRUCTIONS:

1. Wash and gently crush the mint leaves to release their aroma.
2. Place the mint leaves in a teapot or heatproof container.
3. Pour boiling water over the mint and let it steep for 5 minutes.
4. Strain into cups and add honey, sugar, or lemon if desired.
5. Serve warm or chilled for a refreshing twist.

### PER SERVING:
Calories: 22 kcal; Fats: 0g; Protein: 0g; Carbs: 6g; Sugars: 6g; Fiber: 0g

# TEA WITH GINGER

**INGREDIENTS:**

- 1 tablespoon (10 g) fresh ginger
- 2 cups (500 ml) boiling water

**INSTRUCTIONS:**

1. Add ginger slices to the teapot. Pour boiling water over the ginger and steep it for 10 minutes to extract its flavor.
2. Strain the tea into cups and add fresh lemon juice. Add honey or lemon if desired.

**PER SERVING:**

Calories: 22 kcal; Fats: 0g; Protein: 0g; Carbs: 6g; Sugars: 6g; Fiber: 0g

| 2 Portion | Easy | 5 min | 10 min |
|---|---|---|---|

# INVIGORATING HIBISCUS TEA

**INGREDIENTS:**

- 2 tablespoons (10 g) dried hibiscus petals
- 2 cups (500 ml) boiling water

**INSTRUCTIONS:**

1. Add dried hibiscus petals to a teapot. Pour boiling water over the petals and let steep for 10 minutes. Strain the tea into cups.
2. Add honey if desired. Serve warm or chilled for a refreshing alternative.

**PER SERVING:**

Calories: 20 kcal; Fats: 0g; Protein: 0g; Carbs: 5g; Sugars: 6g; Fiber: 0g

| 2 Portion | Easy | 5 min | 10 min |
|---|---|---|---|

# HEALING CHAMOMILE TEA

**INGREDIENTS:**

- 2 tablespoons (10 g) dried chamomile flowers
- 2 cups (500 ml) boiling water

**INSTRUCTIONS:**

1. Place the dried chamomile flowers in a teapot.
2. Pour boiling water over the flowers and steep them for 5–7 minutes to draw out their natural benefits.
3. Strain the tea into cups. If desired, add honey for sweetness, ginger for immune support, or lemon for a vitamin boost. Serve warm.

**PER SERVING:**

Calories: 18 kcal; Fats: 0g; Protein: 0g; Carbs: 4g; Sugars: 3g; Fiber: 0g

# AVOCADO SANDWICHES

## INGREDIENTS:

- 2 slices of thin bread (whole-grain or your choice)(see p. 70)
- 2 tablespoons (30 g) cream cheese
- 1 medium (100 g) avocado, sliced
- 1 tablespoon (10 g) pumpkin seeds

## INSTRUCTIONS:

1. Start by preparing your bread slices. Lightly toast them in a preheated skillet over medium heat or a toaster oven.
2. Lightly toast the bread slices in a skillet or toaster until crispy.
3. Once toasted, let the bread cool for a minute to prevent the cream cheese from melting when you apply it. Take a knife and spread a thin, even layer of cream cheese on each slice of bread.
4. Then, layer the sliced avocado on top of the cream cheese. Sprinkle pumpkin seeds on top for a finishing touch.
5. Serve the open sandwich immediately.

**PER SERVING:**

Calories: 210 kcal; Fats: 15g; Protein: 5g; Carbs: 15g; Sugars: 1g; Fiber: 5g

| 2 Portion | Easy | 5 min | 15 min |
|-----------|------|-------|--------|

| 2 Portion | Easy | 5 min | 6 min |
|-----------|------|-------|--------|

# KETO BREAD MADE FROM NUT FLOUR

## INGREDIENTS:

- 240 g (1 cup) almond flour
- 120 g (1/2 cup) hazelnut flour
- 60 g (1/4 cup) cashew flour
- 4 large eggs
- 60 ml (1/4 cup) coconut oil
- 15 g (1 teaspoon) baking powder
- 2.5 g (1/2 teaspoon) salt
- 15 ml (1 tablespoon) apple cider vinegar
- 60 ml (1/4 cup) water
- Optional: 2.5 g (1 teaspoon) erythritol or stevia

## INSTRUCTIONS:

1. Preheat the oven to 180°C (350°F) and prepare a loaf pan with parchment paper or a light coating of coconut oil.
2. Combine almond, hazelnut, and cashew flours with baking powder and salt. Whisk eggs, coconut oil, apple cider vinegar, and water until smooth, adding sweetener if desired. Mix wet and dry ingredients to form a batter.
3. Pour into the loaf pan, smooth the top, and bake for 35–40 minutes until a toothpick comes out clean. Cool in the pan for 10 minutes, then transfer to a rack to cool completely before slicing.

**PER SERVING:**

Calories: 150 kcal; Fats: 12 g; Protein: 6 g; Carbs: 4 g; Sugar: 0 g; Fiber: 2 g

# CHAPTER 9
# 28-DAY MEAL PLAN
## WHY A STEP-BY-STEP APPROACH MATTERS

Lowering cholesterol isn't about quick fixes—it's about making sustainable changes that last. Rapid, drastic changes in your diet can strain your body and lead to nutrient imbalances. Instead, a step-by-step approach offers a gentle transition, allowing your body to adapt gradually.

This 28-day meal plan was designed to fit into your life, helping you build lasting, heart-healthy habits without feeling overwhelmed.

## THE SCIENCE BEHIND THE 28-DAY MEAL PLAN

This diet focuses on whole foods, including fiber-rich grains, healthy fats, lean proteins, and plenty of fruits and vegetables. These foods have been proven to help lower LDL cholesterol (the "bad" kind) while boosting HDL cholesterol (the "good" type). Key foods like oats, fatty fish, legumes, and nuts have a proven track record for supporting heart health. Soluble fiber in oats and beans binds to bile acids, helping the body eliminate them, while omega-3 fatty acids in fish actively reduce triglycerides and inflammation.

**Weight management also plays a crucial role — losing even a small excess weight can significantly impact cholesterol levels and cardiovascular health.**

## LONG-TERM HEALTH BENEFITS

While the 28-day meal plan provides quick benefits like improved cholesterol and energy, the long-term advantages are even more critical. Consistently following a heart-healthy diet can help reduce your risk of chronic conditions like heart disease, type 2 diabetes, and stroke.

Better sleep, improved mood, and increased energy are just a few benefits of healthy food choices.

These are your body's natural responses to a diet focused on heart health.

## START YOUR JOURNEY TO A HEALTHY HEART

With this meal plan, you're making a temporary change and investing in a healthier future. The meals are heart-healthy, delicious, and easy to prepare, making it simple to stick to your goals.

Each meal is an opportunity to nourish your body and take another step toward a long, healthy life.

Remember, it's not about being perfect; it's about making small, manageable changes that add up over time. By following this plan, you're laying the foundation for lasting heart health.

## ENJOY THE JOURNEY, AND HERE'S TO YOUR VIBRANT, HEALTHY HEART!

# 5 COMMON MISTAKES & HOW TO AVOID THEM

## 1. CUTTING OUT ALL FATS

**The mistake:** Believing that all fats are harmful and eliminating them.

**Why it matters:** Your body needs healthy fats for hormone production, brain function, and nutrient absorption. Going fat-free often leads to relying on processed, low-fat foods filled with added sugars and artificial ingredients—which can raise triglycerides and negatively affect heart health.

**The more brilliant move:** Focus on healthy fats like olive oil, avocados, fatty fish, flaxseeds, and nuts. These unsaturated fats help raise HDL (good cholesterol) and lower LDL (bad cholesterol), promoting cardiovascular balance.

## 2. SKIPPING PROTEIN OR REPLACING IT WITH TOO MANY CARBS

**The mistake** is reducing animal-based foods and replacing them with refined carbohydrates like white bread, pasta, or sugary snacks.

**Why it matters:** Refined carbs can increase triglyceride levels and contribute to insulin resistance, especially if consumed excessively.

**The more brilliant move:** Choose plant-based proteins like legumes, tofu, quinoa, and lentils, or lean animal proteins such as skinless poultry, fish, and egg whites. These support muscle maintenance and help you feel full without spiking your blood sugar.

## 3. NOT READING FOOD LABELS CAREFULLY

**The mistake:** Assuming that "low-fat" o "cholesterol-free" means heart-healthy.

**Why it matters:** Many packaged foods labele "low-fat" or "heart healthy" may still contain tran fats, excess sodium, or hidden sugars, which ca sabotage your progress.

**The more brilliant move:** Always read th ingredient list and nutrition facts. Look for food low in saturated fat, added sugars, and sodiun Avoid anything with "partially hydrogenated oils which indicate the presence of trans fats.

## 4. FORGETTING ABOUT FIBER

**The mistake:** Focusing only on reducing fat an cholesterol intake while overlooking fiber.

**Why it matters:** Soluble fiber plays a key role i heart health by binding to cholesterol in th digestive tract and helping to eliminate it.

**The more brilliant move:** Load your plate wit fiber-rich foods like oats, barley, beans, lentil apples, pears, and vegetables. Aim for at least 25–3 grams of fiber daily to support cholesterol reductio and digestive health.

## 5. EXPECTING INSTANT RESULTS

**The mistake:** Giving up too early when cholester numbers don't improve overnight.

**Why it matters:** Lowering cholesterol is a gradua process, and it takes consistency over weeks or eve months to see measurable changes.

**The more brilliant move:** Be patient with yoursel Stick to the plan, stay active, and keep your stress i check. Over time, your efforts will pay off with bett numbers and more energy. Remember—this is a long term investment in your heart and your future.

Mistakes are part of the process, but awareness your most excellent tool. I've seen firsthand ho minor adjustments—done consistently — ca transform health and restore vitality.

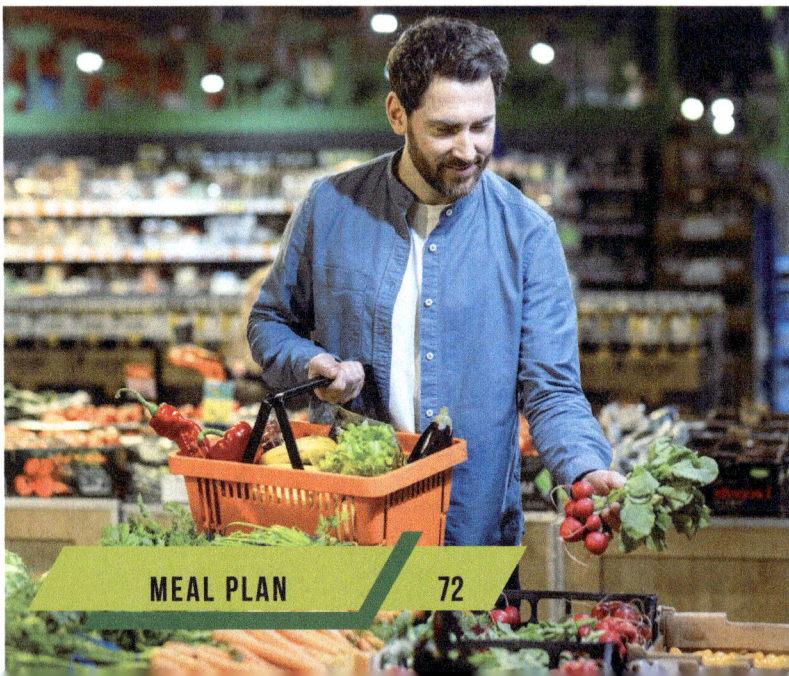

MEAL PLAN 72

### ONE WISE CHOICE, ONE DELICIOUS RECIPE, AND ONE HEALTHY DAY AT A TIME!

# SMART SWAPS: HEART-HEALTHY SUBSTITUTIONS

One key to long-term success on a low-cholesterol diet is flexibility. Eating for your heart doesn't mean giving up the meals you love — it's about making thoughtful, nourishing choices that still bring you joy at the table.

Whether cooking for yourself or the whole family, simple ingredient swaps can help you stay on track without sacrificing flavor or satisfaction.

## EVERYDAY SUBSTITUTIONS FOR A HEALTHIER PLATE

Here are some easy and effective ways to replace common high-cholesterol or high-saturated-fat ingredients with healthier alternatives:

- **Butter    Olive oil or avocado oil**
Rich in monounsaturated fats, these oils are great for cooking and drizzling over vegetables or salads.
- **Whole eggs (daily)    Egg whites or a mix of entire egg + whites**
This helps reduce dietary cholesterol while still providing protein and texture.
- **Cream or heavy sauces    Greek yogurt, mashed avocado, or blended silken tofu**
These options add creaminess with a better nutritional profile.
- **Red meat    Fatty fish (like salmon or mackerel), legumes, or tofu**
You'll reduce saturated fat and gain heart-protective omega-3s or fiber.
- **White rice or pasta    Quinoa, brown rice, or whole-grain pasta**
Whole grains support better blood sugar control and help lower LDL cholesterol.

- **Cheese    Nutritional yeast, low-fat cottage cheese, or fresh mozzarella (in moderation)**
These swaps offer flavor with less saturated fat and sodium.
- **Store-bought snacks    Homemade trail mix, roasted chickpeas, or oat bars**
Avoid trans fats and added sugars by making simple, wholesome snacks at home.

## ADAPTING RECIPES FOR FAMILY & PERSONAL TASTES

Eating healthy becomes easier when everyone at the table enjoys the food. Here are a few ways to personalize your meals while sticking to your heart-healthy goals:

- **Make it modular:** Serve dishes in a "build-your-own" style—like grain bowls or tacos—so everyone can customize their plate using the same healthy base ingredients.
- **Use herbs and spices creatively:** Flavorful food is more satisfying. Let your family choose from different herbs, spice blends, or sauces (like tahini or lemon-garlic dressing) to keep meals interesting.
- **Gradual changes:** If your family is used to richer foods, try blending the old with the new. Mix half white and half whole grain pasta, or start with leaner cuts of meat before fully transitioning to fish or legumes.

With a few smart substitutions and a flexible mindset, you can prepare meals that fit your goals and bring everyone together.

# MEAL PLAN FOR WEEKS 1

| | BREAKFAST | LUNCH | DINNER | SNACK |
|---|---|---|---|---|
| **SUNDAY** | Aromatic Linden Tea p.68 / Delicious Lentil Patties p.14 | Salmon and Vegetable Soup p.36 / Grilled Pork Steak p.46 | Curry with Chickpeas p.57 / Salmon with Lemon Sauce p.38 | Avocado Sandwiches p.70 / Juicy Apples with Almonds p.66 |
| | **Calories: 1817  Fat: 95g  Protein: 96g  Carbs: 145g  Sugar: 43g  Fiber: 33.5g** | | | |
| **MONDAY** | Refreshing Mint Tea p.68 / Milk Berry Buckwheat Porridge p.15 | Yellow Tomato Gazpacho p.33 / Meatballs with Tomatoes p.47 | Fried Cod with Asparagus p.42 / Salad with Goat Cheese, Grapes and Walnuts p.24 | Stuffed Baked Apples p.67 / Soufflé with Raspberries p.63 |
| | **Calories: 1790  Fat: 83g  Protein: 105g  Carbs: 145g  Sugar: 60g  Fiber: 27g** | | | |
| **TUESDAY** | Rosehip Drink p.68 / Roll Salted Salmon and Spinach p.15 | Quinoa with Pistachios p.56 / Grilled Turkey with Salad p.47 | Grilled Cod Fillet p.43 / Wild Rice with Green Beans, Carrots p.58 | Juicy Pear with Honey p.67 / Oatmeal Energy Bars p.64 |
| | **Calories: 1662  Fat: 75g  Protein: 111.5g  Carbs: 150g  Sugar: 48g  Fiber: 24g** | | | |
| **WEDNESDAY** | Tea with Ginger p.69 / Sunny-Side Up Eggs with Pumpkin p.16 | Beans in Tomato Sauce p.55 / Chicken Fillet with Zucchini Grill p.48 | Grilled Mackerel p.41 / Salmon Salad with Pineapple p.25 | Carrot and Orange Smoothie p.63 / Stuffed Baked Apples p.67 |
| | **Calories: 1759  Fat: 82.3g  Protein: 122.6g  Carbs: 141g  Sugar: 83g  Fiber: 25.5g** | | | |
| **THURSDAY** | Invigorating Hibiscus Tea, p.69 / Pancakes with Smoked Salmon p.16 | Grilled Beef Chops p.48 / Soup with Spinach and Meatballs p.33 | Purple Cauliflower Salad, p.25 / Baked Sea Bream p.40 | Juicy Apples with Almonds p.66 / Mini Canapes with Smoked Salmon, Soft Cheese p.62 |
| | **Calories: 1765  Fat: 93g  Protein: 145g  Carbs: 96g  Sugar: 48g  Fiber: 21.5g** | | | |
| **FRIDAY** | Healing Chamomile Tea p.69 / Belgian Cottage Cheese Waffles p.29 | Feta Stuffed Breasts p.50 / Oven Baked Rabbit Legs p.49 | Salad with Avocado and Feta p.26 / Mussels with Lemon and Parsley p.39 | Green Smoothie p.64 / Baked Pear with Cheese p.66 |
| | **Calories: 1808  Fat: 101g  Protein: 119g  Carbs: 100g  Sugar: 48g  Fiber: 22.5g** | | | |
| **SATURDAY** | Rosehip Drink p.68 / Quiche with Chicken p.20 | Baked Chicken Roll p.50 / Beans in Tomato Sauce p.55 | Quinoa with Pistachios p.56 / Salmon Salad with Pineapple p.25 | Juicy Pear with Honey p.67 / Cottage Cheese Cheesecakes p.65 |
| | **Calories: 1677  Fat: 75.5g  Protein: 117.5g  Carbs: 137.5g  Sugar: 47.5g  Fiber: 26g** | | | |

# SHOPPING LIST FOR WEEKS 1

## DAIRY PRODUCTS

- Milk: 390 ml / 13.2 ounces
- Cottage cheese: 670 g / 23.6 ounces
- Heavy cream: 120 ml / 4.1 ounces
- Almond milk: 100 ml / 3.4 ounces
- Cream cheese: 450 g / 15.9 ounces
- Gorgonzola cheese: 120 g / 4.2 ounces
- Blue cheese: 30 g / 1.1 ounces
- Mozzarella cheese: 60 g / 2.1 ounces
- Feta cheese: 80 g / 2.8 ounces

## PROTEIN

- Salmon fillets: 400 g / 14.1 ounces
- Smoked salmon: 350 g / 12.3 ounces
- Chicken breast fillets: 640 g / 22.5 ounces
- Turkey fillets: 400 g / 14.1 ounces
- Beef chops: 600 g / 21.2 ounces
- Rabbit legs: 800 g / 28.2 ounces
- Ground beef or chicken: 600 g / 21 ounces
- Mussels: 900 g / 31.7 ounces
- Sea bream: 300 g / 10.6 ounces
- Eggs: 12 large
- Ricotta cheese: 70 g / 2.5 ounces

## BROTHS AND PASTES

- Chicken or vegetable broth: 2.98 liters / 12 cups

## FRESH HERBS

- Parsley: 40 g / 1.4 ounces
- Basil: 12 g / 1 tablespoon
- Dill: 30 g / 1.1 ounces
- Thyme: 19 g / 2 teaspoons

## SPICES

- Paprika: 30 g / 6 teaspoons
- Garlic powder: 20 g / 4 teaspoons
- Onion powder: 15 g / 3 teaspoons
- Salt and pepper: to taste

## FRUITS AND VEGETABLES

- Mixed leafy greens: 240g / 8 cups
- Spinach leaves: 510g / 4.3 cups
- Purple cauliflower: 150 g / 1 cup
- Pineapple: 120g / 4.3 ounces
- Cherry tomatoes: 450g / 15.9 ounces
- Carrots: 200g / 7.1 ounces
- Cucumbers: 400g / 14.1 ounces
- Apples: 900 g / 31.7 ounces
- Pears: 900 g / 31.7 ounces
- Broccoli: 300 g / 10.6 ounces
- Onions: 300 g / 10.6 ounces

## OILS AND SAUCES

- Olive oil: 295 ml / 1.2 capsules
- Vegetable oil: 20 ml / 4 teaspoons
- Dry white wine: 120 ml / 1/2 cup
- Dijon mustard: 10 ml / 2 tispons
- Lemon Jais: 135ml / 1/2 cup

## NUTS AND SEEDS

- Walnuts: 140 g / 5 ounces
- Pistachios: 60 g / 1/2 cup
- Sliced almonds: 60 g / 2.1 ounces
- Sesame seeds: 10 g / 2 teaspoons
- Chia seeds: 15 g / 1 tablespoon

## OPTIONAL INGREDIENTS

- Honey: 70 ml / 1/4 cup
- Stevia: 8 g / 2 teaspoons

## GRAINS AND LEGUMES

- Lentils: 250 ml / 1 cup
- Gluten-free flour: 48 g / 6 tablespoons
- Buckwheat groats: 80 g / 1/2 cup
- Almond flour: 69 g / 3 teaspoons
- Quinoa: 340 g / 2 cups
- Whole wheat flour: 150 g / 1 1/4 cups
- Rice or oat flour: 120 g / 4.2 ounces
- Wild rice: 185 g / 6.5 ounces
- All-purpose flour: 120 g / 1 cup
- Whole grain oats: 90 g / 1 cup

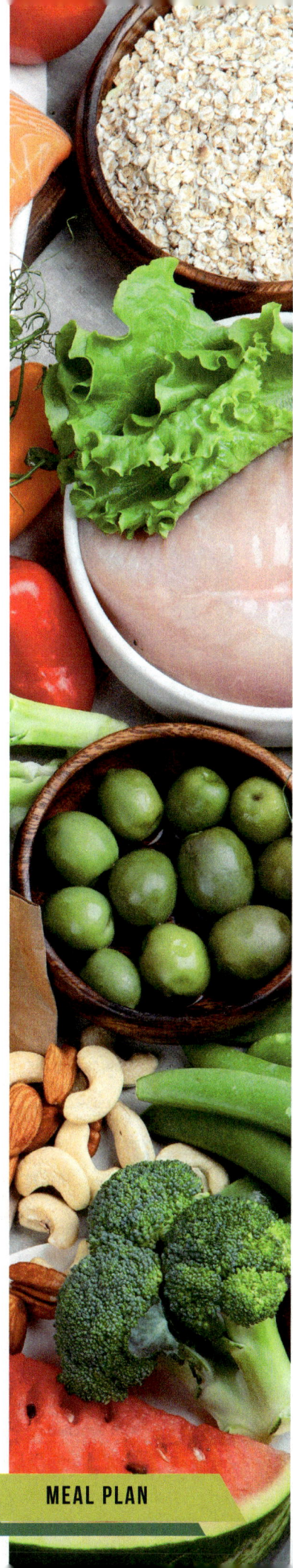

# MEAL PLAN FOR WEEKS 2

| | BREAKFAST | LUNCH | DINNER | SNACK |
|---|---|---|---|---|
| **SUNDAY** | Aromatic Linden Tea p.68 / Pink Pancakes with Strawberries p.22 | Creamy Pumpkin Soup p.34 / Shrimps Salad with Mango p.26 | Bulgur Pilaf with Chicken p.55 / Grilled Salmon with Vegetables p.44 | Soufflé with Raspberries p.63 / Stuffed Baked Apples p.67 |
| | **Calories: 1708 kcal  Fat: 69g  Protein: 84g  Carbs: 200g  Sugar: 93g  Fiber: 30g** | | | |
| **MONDAY** | Healing Chamomile Tea p.69 / Oatmeal with Apples and Pecans p.19 | Grilled Pork Steak p.46 / Beans with Tomatoes and Herbs p.54 | Curry with Chickpeas p.57 / Tuna and Vegetable Salad p.28 | Fruit Salad with Walnuts p.66 / Cottage Cheese Cheesecakes p.65 |
| | **Calories: 1696  Fat: 83.5g  Protein: 78g  Carbs: 165.5g  Sugar: 54.5g  Fiber: 38g** | | | |
| **TUESDAY** | Tea with Ginger p.69 / Eggs with Asparagus and Salmon p.21 | Duck Breast with Sauce p.52 / Salad with Goat Cheese, Grapes and Walnuts p.24 | Shrimps with Lime p.39 / Salad with Feta and Persimmon p. 28 | Green Smoothie p.64 / Mini Canapes with Smoked Salmon, Soft Cheese p.62 |
| | **Calories: 1672  Fat: 98g  Protein: 110g  Carbs: 86g  Sugar: 45g  Fiber: 22g** | | | |
| **WEDNESDAY** | Aromatic Linden Tea p.68 / Chicken and Mushroom Omelet p.18 | Salmon and Vegetable Soup p.36 / Grilled Turkey with Salad p.47 | Turkey with Vegetables p.52 / Salad with Baked Eggplant p.30 | Juicy Pear with Honey p. 67 / Soufflé with Raspberries p.63 |
| | **Calories: 1787  Fat: 84g  Protein: 136.5g  Carbs: 114g  Sugar: 50g  Fiber: 28g** | | | |
| **THURSDAY** | Refreshing Mint Tea, p.68 / Lazy Cottage Cheese Dumplings p.20 | Bean Soup with Tomatoes p.34 / Turkey Stuffed with Spinach p.51 | Salmon with Lemon Sauce p.38 / Chickpea and Spinach Salad with Broccoli p.27 | Oatmeal Energy Bars p.64 / Avocado and Banana Smoothie p.65 |
| | **Calories: 1750  Fat: 77g  Protein: 101g  Carbs: 159g  Sugar: 57g  Fiber: 25** | | | |
| **FRIDAY** | Invigorating Hibiscus Tea p.69 / Pumpkin Rice Porridge p.19 | Duck Breast with Sauce p.52 / Delicious Red Lentil and Vegetable Soup p.35 | Grilled Cod Fillet p.43 / Bulgur Pilaf with Chicken p.55 | Juicy Apples with Almonds p.66 / Mini Canapes with Smoked Salmon, Soft Cheese p.62 |
| | **Calories: 1660  Fat: 63g  Protein: 113g  Carbs: 159g  Sugar: 59g  Fiber: 22.5g** | | | |
| **SATURDAY** | Rosehip Drink p.68 / Savory Mushroom Oatmeal with Poached Eggs p.17 | Oven Baked Rabbit Legs p.49 / Hummus with Vegetable Sticks p.56 | Salmon Salad with Pineapple p.25 / Grilled Salmon with Vegetables p.44 | Carrot and Orange Smoothie p.6 / Avocado Sandwiches p.70 |
| | **Calories: 1701  Fat: 90.3g  Protein: 111.6g  Carbs: 123g  Sugar: 41g  Fiber: 25.5g** | | | |

# SHOPPING LIST FOR WEEKS 2

## DAIRY PRODUCTS

- Low-fat cottage cheese: 540 g / 19 ounces
- Cream cheese: 180 g / 6 ounces
- Fat-free milk: 240 ml / 1 cup
- Plain yogurt (unsweetened): 250 ml / 1 cup
- Soft cream cheese: 150 g / 5 ounces
- Shredded hard cheese: 30 g / 1/4 cup

## PROTEIN

- Skinless chicken breast: 600 g / 21 ounces
- Turkey fillets: 300 g / 10.5 ounces
- Smoked salmon: 400 g / 14 ounces
- Salmon fillets: 830 g / 29 ounces
- Cod fillets: 600 g / 21 ounces
- Rabbit legs: 800 g / 28 ounces
- Duck breast fillets: 300 g / 10.5 ounces
- Eggs: 12 large

## BROTHS AND PASTES

- Chicken or vegetable broth: 1 liter / 4 cups
- Tahini: 30 ml / 2 tablespoons

## OPTIONAL INGREDIENTS

- Sweetener (e.g., stevia): as needed
- Vanilla extract: 5 ml / 1 teaspoon
- Grated fresh ginger: 1 g / 1/2 teaspoon

## SPICES AND FLAVORINGS

- Ground turmeric: 3 g / 1 teaspoon
- Ground cumin: 4,5 g / 1.5 teaspoons
- Paprika: 4 g / 2 teaspoons each
- Garlic powder: 7,5 g / 2.5 teaspoons
- Onion powder: 3 g / 1 teaspoon
- Ground cinnamon: 2 g / 1/2 teaspoon
- Ground nutmeg: 1 g / 1/4 teaspoon
- Ground coriander: 1.5 g / 1/2 teaspoon

## FRUITS AND VEGETABLES

- Apples: 900 g / 31.7 ounces
- Lemon: 240 g / 8.5 ounces
- Orange: 200 g / 7 ounces
- Pineapple: 120 g / 4.3 ounces
- Baby carrots: 300 g / 10.6 ounces
- Broccoli florets: 400 g / 14.1 ounces
- Mini corn: 75 g / 2.7 ounces
- Carrots: 300 g / 10.6 ounces
- Mushrooms: 300 g / 10.6 ounces
- Red bell pepper: 200 g / 7 ounces
- Zucchini: 150 g / 5.3 ounces
- Mixed salad greens: 300 g / 10.6 ounces

## OILS AND SAUCES

- Olive oil: 275 ml / 18 tablespoons
- Lemon juice: 60 ml / 4 tablespoons
- Dijon mustard: 5 ml / 1 teaspoon
- Honey or maple syrup: 87 g / 1/4 cup

## FRESH HERBS

- Fresh parsley: 30 g / 2 tablespoons
- Fresh dill: 30 g / 2 tablespoons
- Fresh basil: 25 g / 5 tablespoons
- Pea sprouts: 15 g / 3 tablespoons
- Radish: 15 g / 3 tablespoons

## NUTS AND SEEDS

- Almonds: 49 g / 1/3 cup
- Pumpkin seeds: 10 g / 1 tablespoon
- Sliced almonds: 60 g / 2.1 ounces

## GRAINS AND LEGUMES

- Bulgur: 300 g / 10.6 ounces
- Slow-cooking oatmeal: 90 g / 1 cup
- Cooked chickpeas: 450 g / 3 cups
- Red lentils: 100 g / 1/2 cup
- Dried white beans: 250 ml / 1 cup

# MEAL PLAN FOR WEEKS 3

| | BREAKFAST | LUNCH | DINNER | SNACK |
|---|---|---|---|---|
| **SUNDAY** | Delicious Lentil Patties p.14 / Refreshing Mint Tea p.68 | Grilled Beef Chops p.48 / Broccoli and Cauliflower Soup p.36 | Purple Cauliflower Salad p.25 / Grilled Fish in Tomato Sauce p.43 | Green Smoothie p.64 / Stuffed Baked Apples p.67 |

**Calories: 1710  Fat: 74g  Protein: 117g  Carbs: 158g  Sugar: 79g  Fiber: 39g**

| | BREAKFAST | LUNCH | DINNER | SNACK |
|---|---|---|---|---|
| **MONDAY** | Aromatic Linden Tea p.68 / Pancakes with Smoked Salmon p.16 | Yellow Tomato Gazpacho p.33 / Turkey Stuffed with Spinach p.51 | Quinoa with Pistachios p.56 / Shrimps Salad with Mango p.26 | Juicy Apples with Almonds p.66 / Avocado Sandwiches p.70 |

**Calories: 1717  Fat: 100g  Protein: 92g  Carbs: 131g  Sugar: 60g  Fiber: 29.5g**

| | BREAKFAST | LUNCH | DINNER | SNACK |
|---|---|---|---|---|
| **TUESDAY** | Invigorating Hibiscus Tea p.69 / Milk Berry Buckwheat Porridge p.15 | Feta Stuffed Breasts p.50 / Soup with Vegetables and Chicken p.32 | Grilled Pork Steak p.46 / Wild Rice with Green Beans, Carrots p. 58 | Baked Pear with Cheese p.66 / Carrot and Orange Smoothie p.63 |

**Calories: 1669  Fat: 78.3g  Protein: 101.6g  Carbs: 145g  Sugar: 65g  Fiber: 21g**

| | BREAKFAST | LUNCH | DINNER | SNACK |
|---|---|---|---|---|
| **WEDNESDAY** | Rosehip Drink p.68 / Belgian Cottage Cheese Waffles p.22 | Curry with Chickpeas p.57 / Baked Chicken Roll p.50 | Beans in Tomato Sauce p.55 / Grilled Mackerel p.41 | Juicy Pear with Honey p.67 / Oatmeal Energy Bars p.64 |

**Calories: 1667  Fat: 72g  Protein: 90.5g  Carbs: 158g  Sugar: 53g  Fiber: 33g**

| | BREAKFAST | LUNCH | DINNER | SNACK |
|---|---|---|---|---|
| **THURSDAY** | Healing Chamomile Tea p.69 / Sunny-Side Up Eggs with Pumpkin p.16 | Shrimps Salad with Mango p.26 / Chicken Fillet with Zucchini Grill, p.48 | Bulgur Pilaf with Chicken p. 55 / Grilled Salmon with Vegetables p.44 | Avocado Smoothie p.65 / Mini Canapes with Smoked Salmon, Soft Cheese p.62 |

**Calories: 1756  Fat: 85g  Protein: 126g  Carbs: 123g  Sugar: 51g  Fiber: 24g**

| | BREAKFAST | LUNCH | DINNER | SNACK |
|---|---|---|---|---|
| **FRIDAY** | Tea with Ginger p.69 / Roll Salted Salmon and Spinach p.15 | Salmon Salad with Pineapple p.25 / Meatballs with Tomatoes p.51 | Fried Cod with Asparagus p. 42 / Salad with Goat Cheese, Grapes and Walnuts p.24 | Juicy Apples with Almonds p.66 / Soufflé with Raspberries p.63 |

**Calories: 1817 kcal  Fat: 103g  Protein: 119g  Carbs: 108g  Sugar: 56g  Fiber: 26.5g**

| | BREAKFAST | LUNCH | DINNER | SNACK |
|---|---|---|---|---|
| **SATURDAY** | Rosehip Drink p.68 / Pink Pancakes with Strawberries p.22 | Turkey with Vegetables p.52 / Soup with Spinach and Meatballs p.33 | Seared Tuna Coated p. 44 / Salad with Goat Cheese, Grapes and Walnuts p.24 | Green Smoothie p. 64 / Stuffed Baked Apples p.67 |

**Calories: 1650  Fat: 74g  Protein: 102g  Carbs: 157g  Sugar: 76g  Fiber: 29g**

# SHOPPING LIST FOR WEEKS 3

## DAIRY PRODUCTS

- Low-fat milk: 300 ml / 1 1/3 cup
- Cottage cheese: 610 g / 2 1/2 cups
- Cream cheese: 360 g / 1 1/2 cups
- Milk: 150 ml / 2/3 cup
- Heavy cream: 120 ml / 1/2 cup
- Ricotta cheese: 70 g / 1/2 cup
- Gorgonzola cheese: 120 g / 1/2 cup
- Blue cheese: 30 g / 2 tablespoons

## PROTEIN

- Shrimp: 200 g / 7 ounces
- Turkey fillets: 300 g / 10.6 ounces
- Chicken breasts/fillet: 720 g / 25.4 ounces
- Beef chops: 600 g / 21.2 ounces
- White fish fillets: 600 g / 21.2 ounces
- Smoked salmon: 150 g / 5 ounces
- Eggs: 9 large
- Almond flour: 60 g / 1/2 cup

## OILS AND SAUCES

- Olive oil: 450 ml / 30 tablespoons
- Lemon juice: 90 ml / 6 tablespoons
- White wine vinegar: 15 ml / 1 tablespoon

## OPTIONAL INGREDIENTS

- Honey or maple syrup: 95 g / 1/3 cup
- Vanilla extract: 5 ml / 1 teaspoon
- Sugar: 5 g / 1 teaspoon

## SPICES AND FLAVORINGS

- Turmeric: 1.5 g / 1/4 teaspoon
- Garlic powder: 20 g / 4 teaspoons
- Onion powder: 10 g / 2 teaspoons
- Smoked paprika: 16 g / 3 teaspoons
- Cinnamon: 2 g / 1/2 teaspoon

## FRUITS AND VEGETABLES

- Apples: 1.5 kg / 53 ounces
- Avocado: 400 g / 14.1 ounces
- Pears: 900 g / 31.7 ounces
- Mango: 150 g / 5.3 ounces
- Cherry tomatoes: 625 g / 22 ounces
- Broccoli: 300 g / 10.6 ounces
- Spinach leaves: 330 g / 5 cups
- Zucchini: 600 g / 21.2 ounces
- Potatoes: 800 g / 28.2 ounces
- Pumpkin: 150 g / 5.3 ounces
- Yellow tomatoes: 600 g / 22 ounces
- Fresh raspberries: 19 g / 0.7 ounces (for 10 berries)
- Fresh blueberries: 20 g / 0.7 ounces (for 20 berries)
- Grapes: 120 g / 4.25 ounces
- Figs: 75 g / 2.65 ounces
- Cranberries: 40 g / 1/4 cup

## FRESH HERBS

- Fresh parsley: 60 g / 1/4 cup
- Fresh mint leaves: 10 g / 2 tablespoons
- Fresh basil: 15 g / 1/4 cup

## BROTHS AND PASTES

- Vegetable broth or water: 1.9 liters / 8 cups

## NUTS AND SEEDS

- Walnuts: 60 g / 1/2 cup
- Almonds: 2.8 g / 0.1 ounces
- Chia seeds: 39 g / 3 tablespoons
- Pumpkin seeds: 10 g / 1 tablespoon

## GRAINS AND LEGUMES

- Buckwheat groats: 80 g / 1/2 cup
- Lentils: 250 ml / 1 cup
- Quinoa: 170 g / 1 cup
- Wild rice: 185 g / 1 cup
- Gluten-free flour: 16 g / 2 tablespoons
- Oat flour: 60 g / 1/2 cup
- Rice or oat flour: 120 g / 4.2 ounces

# MEAL PLAN FOR WEEKS 4

| | BREAKFAST | LUNCH | DINNER | SNACK |
|---|---|---|---|---|
| **SUNDAY** | Tea with Ginger p.69 / Eggs with Asparagus and Salmon p.21 | Feta Stuffed Breasts p.50 / Grilled Pork Steak p.46 | Salmon Salad with Pineapple p.25 / Salad with Avocado and Feta p.26 | Carrot and Orange Smoothie p.63 / Cottage Cheese Cheesecakes p.65 |
| | **Calories: 1699  Fat: 101.8g  Protein: 130.6g  Carbs: 74.5g  Sugar: 41.5g  Fiber: 17g** | | | |
| **MONDAY** | Invigorating Hibiscus Tea p.69 / Quiche with Chicken p.20 | Creamy Pumpkin Soup p.34 / Duck Breast with Orange Sauce p.52 | Grilled Cod Fillet p.43 / Wild Rice with Green Beans, Carrots p.58 | Juicy Pear with Honey p.67 / Soufflé with Raspberries p.63 |
| | **Calories: 1812  Fat: 79g  Protein: 115.5g  Carbs: 175g  Sugar: 54g  Fiber: 29g** | | | |
| **TUESDAY** | Healing Chamomile Tea p.69 / Lazy Cottage Cheese Dumplings p.20 | Beans in Tomato Sauce p.55 / Meatballs with Tomatoes p.47 | Grilled Mackerel p.41 / Salmon Salad with Pineapple p. 25 | Oatmeal Energy Bars p.64 / Avocado and Banana Smoothie p.65 |
| | **Calories: 1706  Fat: 82g  Protein: 114g  Carbs: 134g  Sugar: 57g  Fiber: 18g** | | | |
| **WEDNESDAY** | Aromatic Linden Tea p.68 / Milk Berry Buckwheat Porridge p.15 | Bean Soup with Tomatoes p.34 / Grilled Turkey with Salad p.47 | Bulgur Pilaf with Chicken p.55 / Grilled Salmon with Vegetables p.44 | Fruit Salad with Walnuts p.66 / Stuffed Baked Apples p.67 |
| | **Calories: 1730  Fat: 63g  Protein: 104g  Carbs: 195g  Sugar: 85g  Fiber: 33g** | | | |
| **THURSDAY** | Pumpkin Rice Porridge p.19 / Tea with Ginger p.69 | Meatballs with Tomatoes p.47 / Grilled Beef Chops p.48 | Fried Cod with Asparagus p.42 / Salad with Goat Cheese, Grapes and Walnuts p.24 | Green Smoothie p.64 / Mini Canapes with Smoked Salmon, Soft Cheese p.62 |
| | **Calories: 1812  Fat: 101g  Protein: 109g  Carbs: 120g  Sugar: 48g  Fiber: 26g** | | | |
| **FRIDAY** | Rosehip Drink p.68 / Chicken and Mushroom Omelet p.18 | Oven Baked Rabbit Legs p.49 / Delicious Red Lentil and Vegetable Soup p.35 | Purple Cauliflower Salad p.25 / Grilled Fish in Tomato Sauce p.43 | Juicy Apples with Almonds p.66 / Avocado Sandwiches p.70 |
| | **Calories: 1757  Fat: 89g  Protein: 127g  Carbs: 103g  Sugar: 44g  Fiber: 26.5g** | | | |
| **SATURDAY** | Refreshing Mint Tea p.68 / Savory Mushroom Oatmeal with Poached Eggs p.17 | Feta Stuffed Breasts p.50 / Quinoa with Pistachios p.56 | Grilled Cod Fillet p.43 / Wild Rice with Green Beans, Carrots p.58 | Carrot and Orange Smoothie p.63 / Baked Pear with Cheese p.6 |
| | **Calories: 1936  Fat: 88.3g  Protein: 130.6g  Carbs: 180g  Sugar: 62g  Fiber: 24g** | | | |

# SHOPPING LIST FOR WEEKS 4

## DAIRY PRODUCTS

- Cottage cheese: 680 g / 2 3/4 cups
- Ricotta cheese: 140 g / 1 cup
- Soft cream cheese: 150 g / 5 ounces
- Grated Parmesan cheese: 70 g / 1/2 cup
- Goat cheese: 100 g / 3.5 ounces
- Feta cheese: 80 g / 1/2 cup
- Heavy cream: 120 ml / 1/2 cup
- Fat-free milk: 240 ml / 1 cup
- Almond milk: 120 ml / 1/2 cup

## PROTEIN

- Eggs: 17 large
- Chicken breasts: 940 g / 33 ounces
- Smoked salmon: 513 g / 18 ounces
- Salmon fillets: 600 g / 21 ounces
- Cod fillets: 1.2 kg / 8 pieces
- Ground chicken: 900 g / 2 lbs
- Rabbit legs: 800 g / 4 pieces
- Turkey fillets: 400 g / 4 pieces
- Pork tenderloin steaks: 450 g / 4 pieces

## BROTHS AND PASTES

- Vegetable broth: 1.48 liters / 6 cups
- Chicken broth (low-sodium): 500 ml / 2 cups

## FRESH HERBS

- Fresh parsley: 60 g / 1/4 cup
- Fresh dill: 30 g / 2 tablespoons
- Fresh basil leaves: 25 g / 5 tablespoons
- Fresh thyme leaves: 15 g / 1 tablespoon

## SPICES AND FLAVORINGS

- Paprika: 31 g / 6 teaspoons
- Garlic powder: 51 g / 10 teaspoons
- Onion powder: 15 g / 3 teaspoons
- Ground nutmeg: 1 g / 1/4 teaspoon
- Ground coriander: 1.5 g / 1/2 teaspoon
- Dried oregano: 2 g / 1/2 teaspoon
- Ground cumin: 2.5 g / 1/2 teaspoon

## OPTIONAL INGREDIENTS

- Honey or maple syrup: 110 ml / 4 tablespoons
- Vanilla extract: 10 ml / 2 teaspoons
- Sweetener (e.g., stevia): 10 ml / 2 teaspoons

## FRUITS AND VEGETABLES

- Apples: 1.8 kg / 63.5 ounces
- Pears: 900 g / 31.7 ounces
- Bananas: 240 g / 8.5 ounces
- Oranges: 500 g / 17.6 ounces
- Grapes: 120 g / 4.25 ounces
- Mango: 120 g / 1/2 cup
- Fresh strawberries: 48 g / 1.7 ounces
- Fresh raspberries: 35 g / 2 tablespoons
- Fresh blueberries: 30 g / 2 tablespoons
- Cherry tomatoes: 825 g / 5 1/2 cups
- Broccoli: 450 g / 15.9 ounces
- Cauliflower: 675 g / 23.8 ounces
- Baby carrots: 450 g / 15.9 ounces
- Green peas: 75 g / 1/2 cup
- Radicchio: 60 g / 1/2 cup
- Baby spinach: 490 g / 8 cups
- Arugula: 100 g / 2 cups
- Carrots: 580 g / 3 1/2 cups
- Cucumber: 200 g / 7.1 ounces

## OILS AND SAUCES

- Olive oil: 510 ml / 34 tablespoons
- Lemon juice): 90 ml / 6 tablespoons
- Almond butter: 64 g / 1/4 cup
- Balsamic vinegar: 45 ml / 3 tablespoons
- Apple cider vinegar: 5 ml / 1 teaspoon

## NUTS AND SEEDS

- Chopped walnuts: 150 g / 1 1/4 cups
- Almonds: 35 g / 1/4 cup
- Chia seeds: 35 g / 3 tablespoons
- Pumpkin seeds: 10 g / 1 tablespoon
- Sesame seeds: 10 g / 2 teaspoons

## GRAINS AND LEGUMES

- Buckwheat groats: 80 g / 1/2 cup
- Wild rice: 185 g / 1 cup
- Whole grain oats: 180 g / 2 cups
- Almond flour: 95 g / 1/2 cup + 3 teaspoons
- Rolled oats: 90 g / 1 cup
- Bulgur: 150 g / 5.3 ounces
- Dried white beans: 250 ml / 1 cup
- Red lentils: 100 g / 1/2 cup

# CONCLUSION
## HERE'S TO YOUR HEALTHIER FUTURE

By picking up this book and committing to your health, you've already taken a decisive step toward a stronger heart, a clearer mind, and a more energized life. This journey is more than a die t — it's a shift in how you treat your health, habits, and future. You're no longer waiting for "someday" to feel better — you've decided to start now.

And that's incredibly powerful.

### HEALTHY EATING IS EMPOWERING, NOT RESTRICTIVE

With every heart-friendly choice—swapping butter for olive oil, choosing whole grains, or simply taking a few extra minutes to prepare something nourishing—you're building a new foundation of self-care. You're not following a diet.

You're designing a lifestyle that supports the best version of yourself!

### YOU'RE SET UP FOR SUCCESS

The 28-day meal plan included in this book wasn't just thrown together—it was carefully crafted to make your journey feel doable, enjoyable, and effective. With weekly shopping lists, practical tips, and flavorful recipes, you'll never be left wondering what to eat or how to prepare it. Think of this plan as your roadmap.

### YOU'RE NOT ALONE—I'M WITH YOU EVERY STEP

I didn't write this book to share information. I wrote it because I've been where you are. I've faced the same questions, health worries, and desire for something better.

I know what it feels like to want change and not know where to start. That's why this book exists.

Through every busy morning and every quiet dinner, I'm with you. I've walked this road and know the difference a steady, supportive, heart-healthy routine can make. You don't need to be perfect—you must keep going, one choice at a time.

### STAY CONSISTENT — YOU'VE GOT THIS

I believe in you. I'm proud of your choice—for yourself, your health, and your future. And I want you to remember: the tools are in your hands now. You have everything you need to thrive. Here's to cooking with love, eating joyfully, and living with heart!

### YOU'VE GOT EVERYTHING YOU NEED — NOW TRUST YOURSELF AND KEEP MOVING FORWARD!

*With heartfelt support on your journey,*
*Danny Gibson!*

Printed in Dunstable, United Kingdom

64577707R00047